The UNITED STATES

Its Past, Purpose, and Promise

Part 1 Discovery to the Civil War

Diane Hart

First Discovery

13 Colonies

Revolutionary War

Constitution

Civil War

Reconstruction

GLOBE FEARON
Pearson Learning Group

Globe Fearon Social Studies Books

The UNITED STATES
  Its Past, Purpose, and Promise
    Part 1—Discovery to the Civil War
    Part 2—Industrialization to the Present

Foundations U.S. History

Pacemaker Curriculum U.S. History

Our Century Magazines

Freedom Fighters

Active Learning in Social Studies

African American Experience

African Americans in U.S. History

Hispanics in U.S. History

Acknowledgments: We would like to thank the following people for their time and generosity: Bryan Headley, Photo Researcher: Gordon Fullmer, Case-International; Frank Norick, Principal Museum Anthropologist, and Eugene Prince, Museum Photographer, Lowie Museum of Anthropology, University of California, Berkeley; Barbara Robinson, Education Director, Massachusetts State Archives; Joyce Lee and Betty Odabashian, Schomberg Center for Research in Black Culture, The New York Public Library; and John Anderson, Photograph Archivist, Texas State Archives.

ISBN 0-835-94855-2

Printed in the United States of America
  6 7 8 9 10 11 12   06 05 04

1-800-321-3106
www.pearsonlearning.com

Discovery to the Civil War

Contents

First Discovery
40,000–20,000 B.C.

1607–1733
13 Colonies

Revolutionary War
1776–1783

1788
Constitution

Civil War
1861–1865

1865–1877
Reconstruction

Introduction

Imagine this:

It's the fourth of July! You, your family, your friends, and the people of your town are celebrating in a park. You swim, play baseball, listen to music, dance, talk, eat. Everyone has brought food to share: hamburger; fried chicken; *teriyaki*; B-B-Q ribs; corn-on-the-cob; hotdogs, *kielbasi*, *salami*, and other sausages; *pita*, *tortillas*, and other breads; salads and fruits; cakes and cookies—foods from around the world. That night, fireworks light up the sky.

The fourth of July marks an important event in America's history—the beginning of the United States of America. America's history is the story of events like that. It is also the story of the people of America.

The nation began more than 200 years ago. But America's history began thousands of years before that, when the first people came to America. Much later, other people came. They came from different countries. They were of different

Discovery to the Civil War

races. They worshipped in different religions. But they all became Americans. They made America what it is.

In the next several weeks, you will be reading Part 1 of a history of the United States. You will learn about the beginnings of America. You will learn how Americans fought a war to start a nation, and how they set up a government based on freedom and equal rights.

You will learn how the new United States began to pull apart, and how Americans fought a war to keep it united. You will also learn how Americans, all through the nation's history, have worked to make the nation "more perfect."

As you read about America's history, you will get a better understanding of your country today. You'll better understand the important ideas that your nation is based on. And you'll find it easier to understand events that are happening *now*.

American history is not over. It is still being made. And you are part of it.

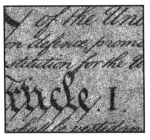

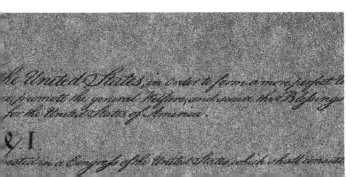

unit 1 A New Land

Somewhere in Asia—20,000 B.C.

It is summer, but frost covers the ground. Inside a cave, a hunter and his family huddle together to keep warm. They wear the skins and fur of animals, but they are still cold. And they are hungry.

The hunter has been hunting for days. But he has not seen a single animal. He has brought no food back to his family.

Once long ago, hunting was good. The land was warm. Many plants grew, and game such as deer and buffalo roamed over the land.

But the climate changed. The air turned cold. Fierce storms covered the land with snow and ice. When summer came, the cold did not go away. The animals became hard to find.

The hunter knows he and his family must leave this cold land or they will starve.

The hunter thinks of stories his people tell of a place far away. They call it the New Land. The New Land is green and warm, full of game. Many of the hunter's people have left to find the New Land. The hunter and his family must leave to find it too.

"To reach the New Land, walk toward the rising sun," the old stories say. "You must walk for many days."

The journey is long and hard for the hunter and his family. Winter comes and they walk across lands heavy with snow and ice. Then summer comes, and they reach a sea. They walk along the side of the sea for miles.

Then the hunter notices that the air is not so cold. In the distance, he sees grass. He sees animals grazing on the grass. The hunter and his family have reached the New Land. Here they can make a new life.

In Our Time

The story shows how the first people *may* have come to America. Historians are not sure who the first Americans were or where they came from. But many believe that the first Americans were hunters who came from Asia thousands of years ago.

Many people still come to America today. They come from many different countries. They leave those countries for many different reasons.

Who are some of the people who come to America today? Where do they come from?

	End of last ice age		Columbus in New World		Jamestown founded		Georgia founded
40,000–20,000 B.C.	10,000 B.C.	1000 A.D.	1492	1519–1522	1607	1620	1733
People in America		Vikings in Newfoundland		Magellan's trip around the world		Plymouth founded	

Chapter 1 The First Americans

For hundreds of thousands of years, no people lived in America. But there was life in America. Forests and grasslands covered large areas. Many kinds of birds and animals lived on the land. Fish filled the rivers and lakes.

And then the first people came.

- Who were the first people to come to America?
- Who are the descendants of the first Americans?
- How did the descendants of the first Americans live in the different parts of America?

Key Words   You will be using these words in this chapter. Look them up in the glossary at the back of this Part 1.

adapt	**artifact**
archeologist	**descendant**

Lowie Museum of Anthropology, University of California, Berkeley

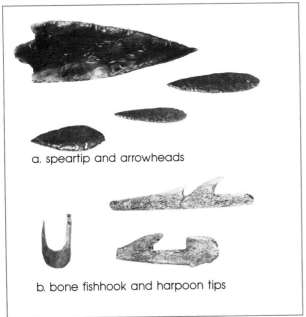

a. speartip and arrowheads

b. bone fishhook and harpoon tips

These artifacts were found in North America. Tools and weapons like these are found in the remains of ancient villages and campsites. Such artifacts help archeologists learn how people in those villages lived.

The Asian Hunters

Who were the first Americans? Where did they come from? When did they come?

Because the first Americans came so long ago, we don't know the definite answers to those questions. But scientists and historians have come up with *theories*, or explanations, about the first Americans.

One theory is this: The first Americans were hunters who came from Asia between 20,000 and 40,000 years ago.

The Asian hunters lived in **prehistoric** times. They lived before people learned to write and keep records. (Prehistoric means before recorded history.) Since the hunters left no writings about themselves, how do we know anything about them?

Archeologists are scientists who study prehistoric people. They look for *evidence* (clues) about people who lived long ago. One kind of evidence is bones found buried in old graves. Other kinds are *artifacts* such as prehistoric weapons, tools, and the remains of ancient villages and campsites. Archeologists and historians study the evidence. Then they develop ideas of what the people were like and how they lived.

Archeologists have found bones and artifacts in Asia that are over 20,000 years old. By studying those bones and artifacts, archeologists have learned this about the Asian hunters: The hunters followed big game animals. They lived in caves or built camps. They made weapons out of stone, bone, and wood.

Looking Back
1. Who do many historians think were the first people to come to America?
2. How do historians know anything about prehistoric people?

Coming to America

Thousands of years ago, the world had several *ice ages*—periods of time when the climate was very cold and thick sheets of ice covered much of the earth. Scientists believe that the climate in Asia changed. It became very cold. Grass and other plants could not live in the bitter cold climate. The animals began to move away, searching for food. They wandered into lands that had a warmer climate where plants could grow.

The Asian hunters were *nomads*—people who move from place to place in search of food. They probably hunted by following herds of animals. When the animals left the cold land, the hunters followed them to the warmer areas.

The Land Bridge

Look at the map at the top of the page. Find the part of North America that is closest to Asia. (Today, we call that area Alaska.) Notice the narrow strip of ocean, between Alaska and Asia.

Scientists believe that the strip of ocean—the Bering Strait—was dry land during the ice ages. That land formed a kind of bridge that linked Asia to North America. They think the land bridge may have been about 1000 miles wide. Scientists believe that the Asian hunters walked over this bridge, following after the animals they hunted.

Looking Back

1. Why did the first people probably come to America?
2. How did the first people probably get to America?
3. Today, people still leave their lands to come to America. What are their reasons for leaving?

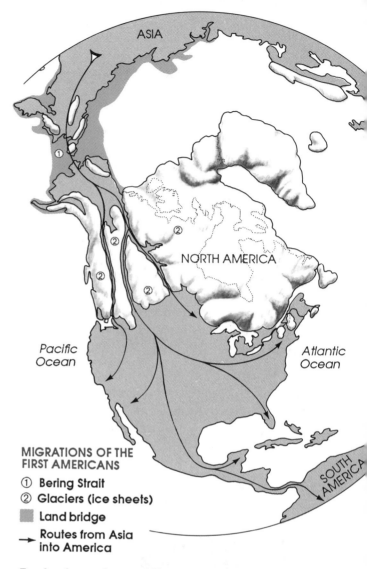

MIGRATIONS OF THE FIRST AMERICANS

① Bering Strait
② Glaciers (ice sheets)
▨ Land bridge
→ Routes from Asia into America

Early American Life

Archeologists believe that the first people to come to America lived as they had in their homeland: They hunted big game animals. They moved from place to place following herds of animals.

The children and grandchildren of those first Americans also became hunters and nomads. They and their children and grandchildren followed herds of animals farther into America. After thousands of years, their **descendants** had spread throughout North and South America. Today we call the descendants of the first Americans **American Indians** and **Eskimos**. (Another name for American Indians is **Native Americans**.)

Adapting to the Land

The early Americans probably were all nomads and hunters until about 10,000 years ago. Then the last ice age ended. The earth became warmer. As the ice and snow melted, the level of the oceans rose. The land bridge disappeared beneath the rising water. The big game animals that had lived during the ice ages died out.

The land in America began to change in many different ways. Some areas continued to be cold and icy. But other areas warmed up. Large forests began to grow in some of those warm areas. Miles of grassy land covered others. And some places became so warm and dry that the lands became deserts.

To survive such changes, Native Americans had to *adapt* to the land they lived on and to its climate. Let's look at how four different groups adapted in four different areas.

The Eskimo

One group of first Americans settled in parts of what is now Alaska. The land was frozen and covered with snow for most of the year. Winters were very long, and summers were very short. We know those people as Eskimos. Their descendants spread into Canada and Greenland.

Eskimos survived mainly by hunting. During the long winter, they hunted sea animals such as walrus, seals, fishes, and whales. During the short summer, they hunted caribou and moose.

Eskimos adapted in remarkable ways to the cold climate. To move across the snow and ice, they made light sleds. They trained dogs to pull the sleds. To hunt at sea, they built *kayaks* and *umiaks*—boats made of animal skins. They learned to build a special kind of house with hard snow. They called their houses *igloos*.

Many of America's early historians were artists. This U.S. postage stamp honors Frederic Remington (1861–1909), who painted many pictures of Native Americans.

The Eastern Woodlands People

After the ice ages, thick forests grew over most of the eastern part of North America. We call that part of North America the **eastern woodlands.** The eastern woodlands stretched from the border of Canada to the Gulf of Mexico.

Many Indian peoples lived in the eastern woodlands, including the Iroquois, Creek, and Seminole. The Indians hunted deer, fished in lakes and streams, and gathered nuts and berries to eat. They also learned to plant corn, beans, and squash. They lived in villages near their cornfields. In the North, the Indians cut down logs and gathered bark for houses. Some tribes built round huts covered with sheets of bark to protect them from the cold. The **Iroquois** built large wooden buildings called *long houses.* Some long houses were 100 feet long. Several families lived together in one house.

The climate in the South was warm. Indians there built homes that could keep them cool. The **Seminoles'** huts had grass roofs. They had raised floors and no walls so cool air could blow through.

Looking Back
1. What do we call the descendants of the first Americans?
2. Why did the descendants have to adapt to a new way of life?
3. How were the lives of Eskimos and eastern woodlands people different?

The Plains people hid under wolf skins and crawled close to buffalos they hunted. This scene was recorded by George Catlin (1796-1872). He shows himself sketching, under the wolf skin at right.

The Plains People

The central area of North America was made up of thousands of miles of flat land. After the ice ages, grass grew thickly on that flat land. Herds of animals, such as buffalo, roamed over the land.

We call that area of grassy flat land the **Great Plains**. We call the Indians who came to live there the *Plains people*. Some of the early Indian peoples were the Missouri, Kansa, Wichita, Omaha, and Iowa. Some Indians that came later were the Blackfeet, Sioux, Comanche, and Cheyenne.

The Plains people grew corn, squash, and beans. They were also skillful hunters. They hunted the buffalo for almost everything they needed. They used buffalo meat for food. They used the buffalos' bones and horns for tools. They also used the buffalos' skins for blankets and clothes.

The Plains people lived in *tepees*— round tents made of buffalo skin. When the buffalo herds moved across the Plains, the Plains people took down their tepees and moved with them.

The Desert People

Other Native Americans lived in the southwest part of America, in what we now call Arizona, New Mexico, and southern Utah. The weather there was hot and dry, and the land had very little water. Most of the land was desert. Game animals and food plants were hard to find.

The people who lived in the Southwest learned to farm to survive. Those people were called **Anasazi**. They built dams and irrigation canals and turned desert land into farmland. The Anasazi are sometimes called *cliffdwellers*. That's because they lived in the cliffs of many canyons in the Southwest. They built tall buildings into the sides of the cliffs. The buildings were made up of many dwellings, or apartments. The Anasazi also wove cloth and made baskets and pottery.

The Anasazi disappeared. But others took their place, like the **Pueblo**. The Pueblo may have been descendants of the Anasazi. The Pueblo grew corn, beans, cotton, tobacco, and squash.

The Pueblo lived in a kind of town. They built buildings out of stone and *adobe*—clay bricks that were dried in the sun. Like the Anasazi, the Pueblo were skillful weavers, basketmakers, and potters.

Another later group that came into the area was the **Navajo**. They learned to farm and weave from the Pueblo. They lived in *hogans*, round buildings made of wood and earth.

Looking Back

1. How were the lives of Plains people and desert people different?
2. How did the Anasazi turn desert into farmland?

Chapter 1

Review

Facts First

Complete each sentence by choosing the correct ending.

1. The first Americans were probably
   a. sailors from Europe.
   b. hunters from Asia.
   c. farmers from Africa.
2. Historians know about the first Americans by studying their
   a. ancient writings.
   b. bones and artifacts.
   c. records.
3. The first Americans probably reached America by
   a. sailing across the Pacific Ocean.
   b. crossing a land bridge to Alaska.
   c. sailing across the Atlantic Ocean.
4. The children and grandchildren of the first Americans
   a. could not survive in America.
   b. stayed in one place.
   c. spread throughout America.
5. The children and grandchildren of the first Americans are called
   a. Hispanic Americans.
   b. Asian Americans.
   c. American Indians and Eskimos.
6. Eskimos lived mainly by
   a. gathering nuts and berries.
   b. farming.
   c. hunting.
7. Desert people lived mainly by
   a. fishing.
   b. farming.
   c. hunting.

Word Check

Write the meaning of each of these words. Then use each word in a sentence.

adapt   **artifact**
archeologist   **descendant**

Skill Builder

On a map of the United States and Canada, point out where each of these groups lived: Eskimos, eastern woodlands people, Plains people, and desert people. Then describe how each area is different from the others.

Chapter 1 Notes

Read over the chapter. Find answers to these questions:

1. Who were probably the first people to come to America? Where did they come from?
2. How did those people get to America?
3. Where did those people settle in America?
4. How did these groups adapt to the areas in which they settled?
   a. Eskimos
   b. eastern woodlands people
   c. Plains people
   d. desert people

Be a Historian

Suppose an archeologist living in the year 3000 digs up your home.

1. What objects would *not* survive being buried for over a thousand years?
2. What objects would survive?
3. What might the archeologist guess about you and the way you lived from studying those objects?

Bonus

Find out about Native Americans that lived in your area long ago. Then report what you learned.

1. What were the people called?
2. What did the Indians eat?
3. What was their clothing like?
4. What kind of houses did they make?
5. How did they travel from place to place?

Chapter 2 # Europeans Come to America

Vikings sailing from Greenland probably discovered the North American continent around the year 1000.

Library of Congress

By the 1400s, Native Americans were living throughout the two continents of North and South America. As you read in Chapter 1, they had developed many different ways to live.

But the lives of Native Americans would soon change: Across the Atlantic Ocean lay another continent, *Europe.* The people of Europe had become merchants, traders, sailors, and explorers. They were seaching for better routes to the countries they traded with, far across the sea. In time, their ships would bring them to America.

- Who were the first Europeans to land in North America?
- Why did Columbus and other explorers come to America?
- Which European countries sent people to live in America?

Key Words   You will be using these words in this chapter. Look them up in the glossary at the back of Part 1.

colony   legislature
empire   settle

The Discoverers

America was probably discovered by Europeans about the year 1000. At that time, **Vikings** were roving over the oceans in their small ships. The Vikings were also called the **Norse**.

The Vikings lived in Scandinavia, in what is now Norway, Sweden, and Denmark. They were fierce, daring warriors who sailed far across the seas to raid the ships and towns of other countries. They were bold sailors. While other Europeans sailed their ships close to land, the Vikings sailed straight out into the ocean. In the North Atlantic Ocean, they discovered Iceland and Greenland. They *settled* on those two lands.

Vikings Arrive in Newfoundland

Around the year 1000, Vikings from Greenland landed on the coast of North America. A group led by **Leif Ericson** explored the land. Leif Ericson called the new land **Vinland**. Shortly afterward, Vikings settled on Vinland. Today, many historians think that Vinland was Newfoundland, a large island off the coast of Canada.

Native people, probably Eskimos, lived on Vinland. They fought the Vikings who settled there. A few years later, the Vikings ended their settlement and returned to Greenland.

The Vikings made up *sagas* (storytelling songs) about Vinland and the people who lived there. Some of those sagas are still remembered today.

The Viking settlers also left behind stone artifacts and other evidence of a settlement in Newfoundland. That evidence and the old sagas tell us that the Vikings were probably the first Europeans in America.

Columbus Reaches America

By the 1400s, other Europeans were exploring unknown waters. They were looking for a sea route to India and China. Europeans called those countries "the Indies." The Indies were part of the continent of Asia.

The Indies had silk, jewels, and spices. Europeans wanted to buy those things, especially the spices. Spices such as ginger, cloves, and pepper improved the taste of meats and other foods.

Traders reached the Indies by traveling over land. But the journey was long and difficult. Explorers began to look for an easier route by sea. Most of them thought they could reach the Indies by sailing south and then east around Africa. But an Italian sailor named **Christopher Columbus** had a different idea. He believed he could sail *west*, go around the world, and reach the Indies in shorter time.

Columbus persuaded Queen Isabella and King Ferdinand of Spain to provide three ships for his voyage. On August 3, 1492, the **Niña**, the **Pinta**, and the **Santa Maria** set sail from Spain.

On October 12, 1492, Columbus landed on an island in the Caribbean Sea, off the coast of North America. He named the island **San Salvador**. Columbus thought he had discovered an island in the Indies. So he called the people he found there "Indians." But he had actually landed in America—by accident.

Sailing West to Asia

Columbus returned to Europe with news that he had reached Asia, and that he had found unknown lands there. But he still hadn't found the route to the Indies. Other explorers now sailed west like Columbus. They wanted to find a route to the Indies.

In 1497 and 1498, **John Cabot** sailed west from England. He explored the coast of North America, around Newfoundland. He claimed Labrador for England. (John Cabot's real name was Giovanni Caboto. He was an Italian who had been hired by the English to find new routes to Asia.)

In 1513, Spanish explorer **Vasco Nunez de Balboa** landed on Panama. Panama is on the narrow strip of land that links North and South America. Balboa crossed Panama and reached the other side. There, he found an immense ocean. That ocean was the Pacific.

A few years later, a Portuguese sea captain named **Ferdinand Magellan** showed that ships could sail completely around the world. In 1519, he left Spain with five ships and sailed west across the Atlantic. He then sailed around South America and across the Pacific Ocean to Asia.

The voyage was long and full of danger. Magellan and many of his men died before it was over. Only one ship finished the voyage. It left Asia, sailed around Africa, and returned to Spain in 1522. That first journey around the world had taken three years.

Looking Back

1. Who were the first Europeans to discover America?
2. What was Christopher Columbus looking for when he sailed west in 1492?
3. Why did Columbus call the people he found Indians?
4. What did Ferdinand Magellan prove?
5. Today, people continue to learn about new places. What places do people explore?

Cortez and his soldiers fight the Tlascalans, neighbors of the Aztecs. This picture is from a history book that was printed in 1893.

Library of Congress

CORTEZ FACES THE TLASCALANS.

Europeans Explore America

Columbus and other explorers of the new lands believed they were in Asia.

Then an Italian named **Amerigo Vespucci** claimed that the new lands in the West were *not* Asia. He claimed they were a new continent. People gave it the name *America*, after Amerigo Vespucci.

Looking for the Northwest Passage

By 1520, Europeans knew the new lands were not Asia. They knew that the Pacific Ocean lay on the western side of North and South America. The French and English believed that there was a water route *through* North America to the Pacific Ocean. They called that water route the **Northwest Passage**. Many of the first English and French explorers came to North America looking for the Northwest Passage. (The Northwest Passage did not exist.)

In the 1520s and 1530s, Giovanni da Verrazano and Jacques Cartier, two explorers for France, explored the coastline from New York to Canada. Later, Henry Hudson, John Davis, and Martin Frobisher explored the Hudson Bay area for England.

Spanish Conquistadores Look for Wealth

Spanish explorers were called *conquistadores*, or conquerors. Many came to North America looking for riches and adventure.

Juan Ponce de Leon heard Indian legends about a fountain of youth. One sip of its waters would make an old person young again. In 1513, he sailed north from Puerto Rico to find the fountain. He never found it. But he did explore the land we now call Florida.

Hernando Cortez heard stories about the Aztec Indians and their riches. The

Aztecs lived in present-day Mexico. In 1519, Cortez sailed from Cuba and landed in Mexico. The Aztecs welcomed the Spanish as gods. But the Spanish stole the Aztecs' gold and destroyed their temples. The Aztecs fought back but were defeated.

Hernando de Soto heard Indian legends of the Seven Cities of Cibola. The Seven Cities were said to have streets paved with gold. In 1540, de Soto searched from present-day Florida to Oklahoma for the Seven Cities. He discovered the Mississippi River, but he found no gold.

Francisco Vasquez de Coronado left Mexico in 1540 to search for the Seven Cities. He had heard about the Pueblo villages of the Southwest and thought they were the Seven Cities. Coronado found the villages, but no gold. In 1542, he returned to Mexico empty-handed. But in his search, Coronado had explored much of the Southwest. That land became part of the growing Spanish *empire* in America.

Looking Back

1. What were the first English and French explorers seeking in America?
2. What were Spanish conquistadores seeking in America?
3. People today still travel to other lands in search of adventure or riches. What are some adventures or riches they seek?

ROCKY MOUNTAINS

Missouri River

Mississippi River

Ohio River

APPALACHIAN MTS

NEW SPAIN

SPAIN IN NORTH AMERICA 1682

Land claimed by Spain

San Salvador Island

Caribbean Sea

Europeans Settle in America

Wherever Europeans explored, they claimed new lands for their kings. The rulers of Europe hoped to gain wealth and power from North America. In the early 1500s, they began to set up *colonies* in America.

The Spanish Settle in Lands to the South

Spain claimed many Caribbean islands, much of Central and South America, and a large part of North America. In North America, they claimed what is now Florida, Mexico, and Texas. They called their American empire **New Spain**.

Colonists in New Spain were given land for farms, ranches, or mines. The colonists often forced the Indians to do the hard work of mining and farming. The Spanish also brought African slaves to America to work for them. A fortune in gold and silver was sent to Spain from North America.

Catholic priests built *missions* throughout New Spain. The missions were settlements centered around churches. Many Indians lived in the missions and learned the Catholic religion.

Spanish and Indian ways combined to create a new way of life. The Spanish taught the Indians a new language. They introduced the Indians to new foods and to new skills, such as riding horses. The Indians introduced the Spanish to foods, such as corn and chocolate. They showed the Spanish new ways of farming and mining. And Indian words and names of places became part of the Spanish language.

By 1550, Spain controlled the largest empire in North America. The riches of New Spain helped to make Spain the strongest nation in Europe. Other nations, especially France and England, wanted their share of the wealth from North America.

Looking Back

1. Where did the Spanish settle in North America?
2. How did Spain get rich in North America?
3. How was Indian life changed because of the Spanish?
4. What did the Spanish learn from the Indians?

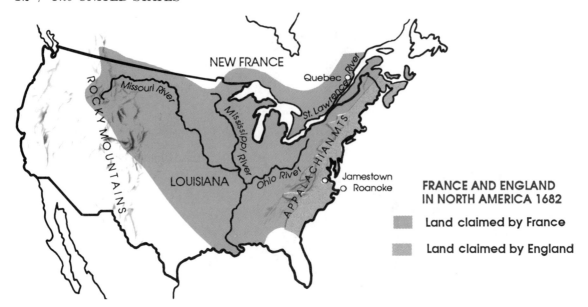

NEW FRANCE

Quebec

St. Lawrence River

Missouri River

Mississippi River

Ohio River

ROCKY MOUNTAINS

APPALACHIAN MTS

LOUISIANA

Jamestown
Roanoke

FRANCE AND ENGLAND
IN NORTH AMERICA 1682

Land claimed by France

Land claimed by England

French Settle in Louisiana and Canada

The first French colonists in America settled in Canada, near present-day Quebec. The French called their settlement **New France**.

The French came to America mainly to get beaver fur. The colonists often traded with the Indians to get the fur.

In 1679–1682, a trader named **Robert de La Salle** traveled from the Great Lakes down the Mississippi River. He claimed the entire Mississippi River Valley for France. La Salle named this vast region Louisiana in honor of the French king, Louis XIV.

The French built forts and trading posts throughout New France and Louisiana. But the number of French settlers in America remained small.

English Settle on the East Coast

In 1585, the first English settlement in America was built on **Roanoke Island**, off the coast of present-day North Carolina. By 1587, over a hundred people were living there. But in 1590, the Roanoke settlers mysteriously disappeared.

In 1607, another group of English settlers settled on Virginia's Chesapeake Bay. They called their settlement **Jamestown**.

The first years at Jamestown were hard. During the first winters, the settlers were saved from starving by the nearby Powhatan Indians.

Then, in 1612, the settlers discovered that tobacco grew well in Jamestown. Tobacco, a native American plant, was becoming very popular in Europe. Jamestown colonists planted it everywhere, even between gravestones. The success of tobacco brought more colonists to Virginia, and more settlements were started.

In 1619, the Virginia colonists elected 22 *burgesses*, or representatives, to the Virginia **House of Burgesses.** The House of Burgesses became the first colonial *legislature* in America. A legislature is a group that makes laws. The House of Burgesses met to make laws for the whole colony.

Looking Back

1. Where did the French settle in America?
2. Where did the English settle in America?
3. Many French and English names for places are still used today in the United States. What are some of them?

Chapter 2

Review

Facts First

Complete each sentence by choosing the correct ending.

1. The first Europeans to discover America were probably the
   a. French.
   b. Vikings.
   c. Spanish.
2. Columbus sailed west across the Atlantic Ocean looking for
   a. the Indies.
   b. the Fountain of Youth.
   c. New Spain.
3. Early English explorers explored the coast of North America seeking
   a. the Northwest Passage.
   b. beaver furs.
   c. the Seven Cities of Cibola.
4. The rulers of Europe built colonies in America to increase their nation's
   a. farmland.
   b. wealth and power.
   c. number of people.
5. Spanish conquistadores in America were seeking
   a. the Northwest Passage.
   b. beaver furs.
   c. riches and adventure.
6. The Mississippi River Valley was claimed by
   a. Spain.
   b. France.
   c. England.
7. The three main European countries to settle first in America were
   a. Italy, Portugal, and Russia.
   b. China, India, and Japan.
   c. Spain, France, and England.

Word Check

Write the meaning of each of these words. Then use each word in a sentence.

colony   **legislature**
empire   **settle**

Skill Builder

Make a timeline of your life. Draw a long line across a sheet of paper.

1. Write the year you were born at the left end of the line.
2. Write the present year at the right end of the line.
3. Divide the timeline into equal periods of years. Label the years.
4. Now think of some things that have happened to you during your life. Write each event and the year it happened at the correct mark on the timeline.

Chapter 2 Notes

Read over the chapter. Find answers to these questions:

1. Who were probably the first Europeans to discover America?
2. What were Columbus and other early explorers trying to do when they reached America?
3. How did America get its name?
4. Why did European rulers begin to set up colonies in North America?
5. Where did these groups settle in North America?
   a. Spanish; b. French; c. English
6. What was the House of Burgesses?

Bonus

The first English settlement in America was on Roanoke Island. Today that settlement is known as the Lost Colony.

Find out more about the Lost Colony at Roanoke. Then report what you learned.

Chapter 3 The English Colonies

This engraving is called "The First Landing of the Pilgrims, 1620."

In 1620, 13 years after the settlement of Jamestown, another group of English people came to America. They came in a small ship called the *Mayflower*. They came to America seeking the right to worship God as they pleased.

Over the next hundred years, many more English people came to America. They came for many different reasons. But all came hoping to find a better life.

By 1733, there were 13 English colonies lining America's eastern shoreline. Those 13 colonies would later become a new nation, the United States of America.

- Why did English settlers come to America?
- Where did the settlers get their ideas about government?
- Why were African slaves brought to the colonies?
- How did the settlers make a living in the different colonies?

Key Words   You will be using these words in this chapter. Look them up in the glossary at the back of Part 1.

democracy	**immigrant**
founded	**self-government**

The New England Colonies

The English *founded* many settlements along the northeastern coast of America. In time, those settlements joined together to form the four colonies of New England. They were **Massachusetts**, **Rhode Island**, **Connecticut**, and **New Hampshire**.

First Settlement at Plymouth

The people who came to America on the *Mayflower* were called the **Pilgrims**. (Pilgrims are people who make a journey for religious reasons.) They had left England to find religious freedom. In England, everyone was expected to believe in the country's official religion and to worship God the same way the king did. The Pilgrims refused to do so. As a result, they were often mistreated because of their beliefs.

Before they left the *Mayflower*, 41 Pilgrim men made an agreement called the **Mayflower Compact**. In the compact, the Pilgrims agreed to form their own government, make laws, and obey those laws. The Pilgrims founded the first English settlement in New England. They called it **Plymouth**.

Massachusetts

In 1630, another group of English people arrived in America. They were called **Puritans**. They settled near present-day Boston. The Puritans also left England because they did not agree with England's official religion.

The Puritans set up their own government. They believed that everyone should follow God's will. So, they passed laws to force everyone to live according to Puritan beliefs.

In 1691, the Pilgrim settlement and the Puritan settlement joined together and formed the colony of Massachusetts. It was the largest colony in New England.

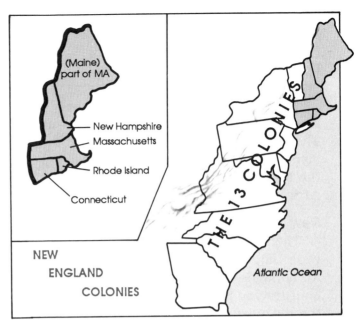

New England / The 13 Colonies / New England Colonies — map showing Maine (part of MA), New Hampshire, Massachusetts, Rhode Island, Connecticut, Atlantic Ocean

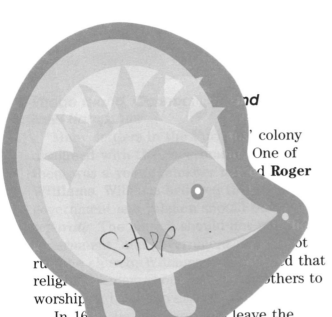

...nd

...' colony
...One of
...d **Roger**
...Williams...

...ot
ru... that
relig... thers to
worship...

In 16... leave the
colony. He... like him founded
new settlements south of Massachusetts.
Anne Hutchinson, a Puritan woman, also
spoke out against the government. She,
too, was driven out of the colony because
of her religious views. She also founded a
settlement south of Massachusetts. In
1647, those settlements became the colony
of Rhode Island. Roger Williams based the
government of Rhode Island on religious
freedom. All who settled there were free
to follow their own religious beliefs.

In 1636, another minister left the
Puritan colony. His name was **Thomas
Hooker**. Hooker and his followers settled
west of Rhode Island. In time, their
settlements became the colony of
Connecticut.

Other colonists moved north to found
new settlements. In 1680, their settlements
became the colony of New Hampshire.

Making a Living in New England

Most New Englanders were farmers
who grew corn, fruit, and vegetables.
Others fished for cod, cut logs in the
forests, or worked as shipbuilders. And
some New Englanders were merchants
who shipped beaver furs and salted cod to
Europe.

Local Self-Government

Most New Englanders lived in small
towns. At the center of each town was a
meeting house where the colonists met to
worship. They also met to help run the
government of their town.

Every month, townspeople gathered at
the meeting house to solve the problems of
the town. Everyone had a chance to
speak. Then the men of the town voted.

In their town meetings, New Englanders
were starting to use some of the ideas of
democracy and *self-government*. In a
democracy, the people choose their leaders
and laws. Under self-government, people
rule themselves; they are not ruled by a
king or his officials.

Those ideas of democracy and self-
government became very important to the
colonists.

Looking Back

1. What were the New England colonies?
2. Why did the Pilgrims and Puritans come
   to America?
3. How did New Englanders make a living?
4. How did New Englanders practice
   democracy and self-government?
5. Which of the New Englanders' ideas
   about freedom and government are still
   important in America today?

The Middle Colonies

The middle colonies were **New York**, **New Jersey**, **Pennsylvania**, and **Delaware**. The settlers in those colonies came from many different places, such as England, the Netherlands, Germany, Ireland, and Africa.

New York and New Jersey

The first settlers in the middle colonies were Dutch. They came from the Netherlands. In the early 1600s, the Dutch built trading posts and settlements throughout the Hudson River Valley. Those settlements became a Dutch colony called **New Netherland**.

In 1664, the English king claimed that all of New Netherland belonged to him. Four English warships were sent to the Dutch settlement of New Amsterdam. The Dutch surrendered to the English without a fight.

The English divided New Netherland into two colonies. They called the northern colony New York. They called the southern colony New Jersey.

Pennsylvania and Delaware

Another religious group in England was the **Quakers**. The Quakers, like the Pilgrims and Puritans, disagreed with England's official religion.

Quakers were often jailed in England because of their beliefs. For example, Quakers believed that war was wrong. So, they refused to fight in the king's army. Quakers saw no need for ministers. They believed each person could understand God's word without a minister's help.

In 1681, an English Quaker named **William Penn** saw a chance to help the Quakers. The King of England, Charles II, owed Penn's father a large sum of money. The king repaid the debt by giving Penn a large area of land in America.

Penn founded a colony on that land. He named it Pennsylvania after his father. Penn attracted Quakers and others by offering land and religious freedom.

In 1682, Penn was given control of Delaware, an area first settled by people from Sweden. Delaware became a separate colony in the early 1700s.

The Bread Colonies

The middle colonies grew rapidly. Many *immigrants* from England, France, Germany, Sweden, Ireland, and other countries settled there.

Most settlers were farmers. They found the soil there good for raising wheat, rye, oats, and corn. Soon, the middle colonies were growing more grain than any other region. They became known as the **bread colonies** because they sold so much wheat to Europe and other American colonies.

Looking Back
1. What were the middle colonies?
2. How did New Netherland become New York and New Jersey?
3. Why did the Quakers leave England for Pennsylvania?
4. Why were the middle colonies known as the "bread colonies"?

The Southern Colonies

Five English colonies developed along the southeastern coast of North America. They were **Virginia**, **Maryland**, **North Carolina**, **South Carolina**, and **Georgia**. Most of them began as **proprietary colonies**. Those were colonies that were owned by a person or a group of persons. Proprietors made money by renting or selling their land to settlers. They also taxed the settlers.

How They Begin

In Chapter 2, you read that Jamestown was the first permanent English settlement in North America. Jamestown was started in 1607 by businessmen. Jamestown was part of the Virginia colony.

The next southern colony founded was Maryland. It was started in 1632 as a proprietary colony. Its owner was **Lord Baltimore**, an English noble. He had been given the land by King Charles I. Lord Baltimore promised religious freedom to Catholic and Protestant settlers.

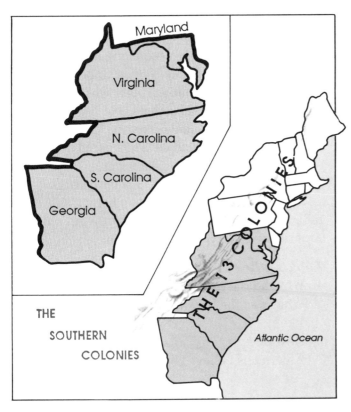

THE SOUTHERN COLONIES

Then the next King of England, Charles II, gave a group of nobles land south of Virginia. The land was called Carolina. Carolina's proprietors planned to make money by renting land to settlers. But settlers wanted to own land, not rent it. The colony grew only after the proprietors offered settlers land of their own. Later, Carolina was divided into North and South Carolina.

Georgia was the last of the 13 English colonies to be settled. Georgia was not set up for profit. Georgia's proprietor, **James Oglethorpe**, wanted a place where England's poor people could make a new life. But Georgia remained small: Few poor people settled there.

Farmers and Planters in the South

Settlers were drawn to the southern colonies by the chance to own land. Most settlers owned small farms. A farm family could raise most of the food they needed. They could also raise a *cash crop*, a crop grown to be sold.

In Virginia and Maryland, farmers raised tobacco as their major cash crop. In the Carolinas, farmers raised rice and *indigo*, a plant used for making blue dye.

The largest farms in the South were **plantations**. They were often hundreds of acres in size. A plantation usually had a large family house, beautiful lawns and gardens, stables, and barns filled with tobacco or rice. Plantation owners, or *planters*, became rich selling their crops in England and elsewhere. Planters often became leaders in colonial legislatures.

Looking Back

1. What were the southern colonies?
2. How did proprietors hope to make money from the colonies they owned?
3. How did most settlers in the South make their living?

America's story is often retold in television stories and movies. These scenes from *Roots*, televised in 1977, show young African Kunta Kinte (*left*) on a slave ship, and (*right*) in America, about to be sold.

Warner Brothers Television Distribution

Servants and Enslaved People

The plantations of the South needed workers. Large numbers of field hands were needed to plant and *harvest* (pick) the crops. Other workers were needed to tend the gardens, care for the horses, and cook and clean for the planters' families.

Indentured Servants

The first plantation workers were **indentured servants**. Most of them came from Europe. The plantation owners paid the cost of their trip to America. In return, the workers agreed to work as servants for a certain number of years. When their time of service ended, they received their freedom. Some also received a small piece of land.

Slavery

As plantations grew larger, the need for workers increased. There were not enough indentured servants. And planters wanted *permanent* workers, workers who would not leave someday. The planters found a solution to their problem—enslaved people from Africa.

In the 1660s, Virginia and Maryland made slavery legal. Other colonies soon followed their lead. By 1672, slave trading was a profitable business in the colonies.

Slave traders bought or kidnapped African men, women, and children. The traders then shipped them in chains to America. Many died of disease on the crowded slave ships.

In America, the slaves were sold as property. Most slaves worked long hours in the fields. Others were trained to be carpenters or blacksmiths. A few worked as cooks or household servants.

Enslaved people had no rights. They had to give up their names. They could be sold from one master to another. Any children they had belonged to their owners.

By 1770, there were almost a half-million slaves in the colonies. For them, America was not a land of freedom.

Looking Back

1. Why did the planters start using slaves?
2. What was the life of an enslaved person like?
3. How does slavery go against what Americans believe?

Chapter 3

Review

Facts First

Read sentences 1–10. Which group of colonies does each sentence describe? Choose your answer from the answer box.

> a. **the New England colonies**
> b. **the middle colonies**
> c. **the southern colonies**
> d. **all 13 English colonies**

1. Pilgrims and Puritans settled here.
2. Quakers settled here.
3. The main crops were tobacco, rice, and indigo.
4. Settlers were attracted by the chance to own their own land.
5. They were the "bread colonies."
6. Fishing and ship building were important here.
7. Slaves were brought here to work on plantations.
8. Most of the settlers were farmers.
9. The settlers held town meetings.
10. Colonists here sold grain to Europe.

Word Check

Write the meaning of each of these words. Then use each word in a sentence.

democracy	**immigrant**
founded	**self-government**

Skill Builder

Make a timeline that shows each event below. Put the events in order. Begin with the year 1607. End with the year 1681.
1620 Pilgrims sail on the Mayflower.
1632 Maryland is founded.
1630 Puritans settle Massachusetts.
1647 Rhode Island becomes a colony.
1681 Quakers settle Pennsylvania.
1607 Jamestown is settled.

Chapter 3 Notes

Read over the chapter. Find answers to these questions:
1. Why did the Pilgrims, Puritans, and Quakers leave England for America?
2. How did the New England colonists use ideas of democracy and self-government?
3. What did most settlers do in the middle colonies? How did that become important to the other colonies?
4. How did most of the southern colonies begin?
5. In what two ways did plantation owners get workers for their huge farms?

Be a Historian

The first settlers came to America over 400 years ago. Today, people are still coming to America. Interview someone who has come to the U.S. from another country. Ask that person these questions:
1. When did you come to the U.S.?
2. What country did you come from?
3. Why did you leave your home?
4. Why did you choose the U.S. as your new home?

Bonus

Find out about one of these important people from America's past. Then report what you learned.

Thomas Hooker	William Penn
Anne Hutchinson	Pocahontas
Massasoit	Captain John Smith
Peter Minuit	Squanto
James Oglethorpe	Roger Williams

Unit 1  Review

What Do You Know?

Complete each sentence by choosing the correct ending.

1. The first Americans were probably
   a. Pueblo people.
   b. Vikings from Greenland.
   c. Asian hunters.
2. We call the descendants of the first Americans
   a. American Indians and Eskimos.
   b. conquistadores.
   c. Pilgrims.
3. Descendants of the first Americans
   a. could not survive in America.
   b. never moved off the land bridge.
   c. spread throughout America.
4. Columbus found America while seeking
   a. a route to the Indies.
   b. the Fountain of Youth.
   c. a place to worship freely.
5. Conquistadores came to America in search of
   a. a route to the Indies.
   b. religious freedom.
   c. riches and adventure.
6. The Pilgrims came to America seeking
   a. gold.
   b. the Northwest Passage.
   c. religious freedom.
7. The settlers of New England got their ideas about government from
   a. Spain.
   b. the Indians.
   c. England.
8. Most people in the 13 colonies
   a. were slaves.
   b. owned plantations.
   c. lived on small farms.

What Do You Think?

Life in a new land is often difficult. The first settlers who arrived in America faced a variety of hardships, such as starvation. In your lifetime, people may begin to settle in space. In what ways do you think life will be difficult for the first space settlers?

Skill Builder

Find out in what years these events happened. Then write them in order.
- Cortez conquers the Aztecs in Mexico.
- Magellan begins his voyage around the world.
- Viking sailors discover America.
- The Pilgrims arrive in New England.
- Columbus lands in America.
- The first arrivals cross the land bridge.

Unit 1 Notes

Look over the unit to find answers to these questions:

1. How do historians think the first people probably came to America thousands of years ago?
2. What did these explorers discover or prove?
   a. Balboa   b. Magellan   c. de Soto
3. What are three different reasons Europeans began to settle in America?
4. Why were Africans brought to America as slaves?

Word Builder

Write a story about one of the groups of people you read about in this unit. Use all the key words listed below.

Key Words

adapt	legislature
artifact	self-government
immigrant	settle

The American Revolution (1776-1783)

Lexington, Massachusetts—April 19, 1775

A man on horseback races into the village. The man is Paul Revere. He has a warning for the villagers: British soldiers are coming!

Moments later, the leader of the village pounds on young William Diamond's door:

"William, wake up! The British are coming through Lexington! Quickly! Bring your drum to the common!"

William snatches up his drum and hurries to the common. It is a grassy field in the center of the village. He strikes his drum again and again, alerting the people of the village. Quickly, villagers gather in the darkness. They carry their muskets.

As the sun rises, William and the other villagers stand waiting. An army of British soldiers in red coats rapidly marches toward them. The Redcoats greatly outnumber the villagers.

"Don't fire unless fired on!" the leader of the villagers shouts to the others. "But if they mean to have war, let it begin!"

For a moment, the common is quiet. Then a single shot cuts through the stillness. British troops and villagers begin firing.

The battle is quickly over. Several villagers lie dead or wounded. Only one British soldier is wounded. The British troops shout victoriously, then march on.

William stares in horror at the scene. The common is covered with the bodies of his friends and neighbors.

"It's not over!" he says angrily to himself. "As long as one Redcoat remains in America, it's not over!"

In Our Time

William Diamond was a sixteen-year-old teenager who fought in the war between Britain and the colonies.

That war is called the **Revolutionary War**, or the **American Revolution**, because the colonies were fighting to *throw out* a government. The war is also known as the **War for Independence** because the colonists were fighting to be free.

Today, Americans still fight for freedom in our country. In what ways do Americans today fight for freedom?

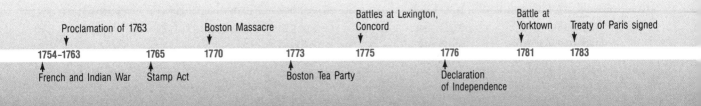

	Proclamation of 1763	Boston Massacre		Battles at Lexington, Concord		Battle at Yorktown	Treaty of Paris signed
1754–1763	1765	1770	1773	1775	1776	1781	1783
French and Indian War	Stamp Act		Boston Tea Party		Declaration of Independence		

Chapter 4 The Colonies Rebel

This U.S. postage stamp, issued in 1925, observes the first battles for liberty.

By 1750, over a million people lived in the British colonies. The colonies were now over a hundred years old. They had grown from small settlements into large colonies of busy villages, towns, plantations, and farms. Although the colonies were ruled by Britain, each colony had its own government. Each colony ran itself.

Then trouble developed between the colonists and Britain. By 1776, many colonists were no longer happy with British rule. They felt that Britain was not treating them fairly. They also felt that Britain was taking away their rights.

- Why did the colonists become unhappy with British rule?
- In what ways did colonists protest against British rule?
- Why did the colonies finally break away from Great Britain?

Key Words   You will be using these words in this chapter. Look them up in the glossary at the back of Part 1.

boycott	**militia**
independence	**repeal**

The Conflict Begins

When the English settled in America, they brought certain ideas about government with them from England. They also brought certain ideas about the rights of people with them.

The Rights of English People

Although a king ruled England, he did not have complete power. That's because the English people had won certain rights. One of those rights was the right to make laws. The king did not make the laws. **Parliament** did. Parliament was the English legislature. Members of Parliament were elected by landowners.

Another important right was a person's right to a trial by jury if accused of a crime. The English government had a system of courts for those trials.

In America, English colonists had the same rights as people in England.

Self-Government in the Colonies

The English government was made up of three parts: a ruler (the king or queen), Parliament, and the courts. Each colony set up a **colonial government** that also had three parts.

One part of the colonial government was the **governor**. He ruled the colony. He was chosen by the king or elected by the colonists.

The second part of the government was the **legislature**. (Sometimes it was called an *assembly*). It made laws, controlled the colonial *militia*, and set taxes. Colonists elected the members of their legislatures.

The third part of the government was the colonial **courts**. All colonists had the right to a trial by jury.

With those colonial governments, the colonists practiced self-government: They governed themselves. By 1754, they had been governing themselves for over a hundred years.

French and Indian War (1754–1763)

In 1753, colonists learned that French troops were building forts in what is now western Pennsylvania. The French claimed the land was French territory. But Virginia claimed the forts were in Virginia territory.

In 1754, Virginia sent troops to build a fort in the territory. A young officer named **George Washington** led those troops. The troops built a fort called Fort Necessity. French troops and Indians attacked and defeated Washington's troops at Fort Necessity. That battle began a war in America known as the **French and Indian War**. That war lasted for almost ten years.

Several Indian tribes sided with the French against the colonists. Together, the French and Indians defeated the colonial and British armies in battle after battle. Then, in 1758, Britain shipped several thousand more troops to America.

In 1759, British forces captured the French city of Quebec. Quebec was the capital of New France. The fall of Quebec was the turning point in the war. Four years later, France asked for peace.

In the peace agreement of 1763, France lost nearly all of its territory in America. Canada and lands east of the Mississippi River were given to Britain. French territory west of the Mississippi was given to Spain. That territory was called Louisiana. Britain also received Florida from Spain.

The Problems of Peace

Britain's victory in the war added new territory to its empire in America. Britain now had a problem: how to defend that huge, new territory.

The Indians of the Ohio Valley had fought beside the French. They did not trust the British who settled there after the war. In 1763, an Ottawa chief named **Pontiac** led an uprising against the British. The Indians destroyed several British forts and settlements. British troops defeated Pontiac. But the uprising convinced the British that it would be dangerous to allow settlers into the new territory.

To stop settlement, Parliament issued the **Proclamation of 1763**. That was a law that colonists could not settle west of the Appalachian Mountains.

The proclamation angered many colonists. The colonists believed they had the right to live where they pleased.

Parliament also decided to send more British troops to America. Thousands of troops were needed to defend the new territory and protect the colonists. But who would pay the costs of feeding and *quartering* (housing) those troops? Parliament decided that the colonists should help pay for the troops.

Parliament also decided the colonists should help pay the costs of the French and Indian War. The British had a huge war debt. They had borrowed large sums of money to fight the war. Parliament wanted the colonists to help repay that debt.

Looking Back
1. List two rights that English people had.
2. Why were English colonists used to making their own decisions?
3. What territory did Britain gain in the French and Indian War?
4. What was the Proclamation of 1763? How did colonists feel about it?
5. How did Parliament decide to pay for British troops in America?
6. *Map work*: Look at a large map of the United States today. Point out the territory covered by the Proclamation of 1763.

Trouble Begins

Between 1764 and 1773, Parliament passed a series of new *acts*, or laws, for the colonies. Most of those acts were tax laws. The tax money would go to the British government to help pay for British troops in America. The money would also help Britain repay its war debt.

Many colonists were angered by the tax laws. They believed the laws *violated*, or went against, their rights.

No Taxation Without Representation

In 1764, Parliament passed the **Sugar Act**. That law forced colonists to pay taxes on goods that they *imported* (brought in) from Britain. Some of those goods were sugar, coffee, and wine. Colonists had not paid taxes on those goods before.

In 1765, Parliament passed the **Stamp Act**. That Act said that special tax stamps had to be put on items such as newspapers, playing cards, and legal papers. The stamps showed that the tax on those items had been paid. The tax stamps raised the price of those items, sometimes from a penny to ten dollars.

The Stamp Act also said that colonists who disobeyed the Act would be tried in special courts. The special courts would not have juries.

The Stamp Act angered the colonists. They believed the Act took away their right to make their own laws. They also believed the Act took away their right to a jury trial.

Many angry colonists began to say, "No taxation without representation!" They meant that Parliament had no right to tax them because the colonists could not elect people to *represent*, or speak for, them in Parliament. The colonists believed that only their elected legislatures had the right to tax them.

The Colonists Protest

People throughout the colonies protested against the Stamp Act. One who spoke out was **Patrick Henry**, a Virginia lawmaker. He made a powerful speech against the tax in the Virginia House of Burgesses.

Colonists calling themselves the **Sons of Liberty** led marches against the Act. They seized and burned the hated stamps in several cities. Women formed groups called the **Daughters of Liberty**. They called upon all women to *boycott* British goods.

Faced with such protest, Parliament gave in. In 1766, it *repealed* the Stamp Act.

The Boston Massacre

Parliament did not give up the idea of raising money in the colonies. In 1767, Parliament passed the **Townshend Acts**. Those acts taxed imported goods such as tea, glass, and paper.

Again the colonists protested. **Samuel Adams** was a member of the Massachusetts legislature. He led protests in Boston. Adams wrote newspaper articles warning colonists that the British were taking away their rights. The Daughters of Liberty organized more boycotts.

This time the British government did not back down. Instead, it tightened its grip on the colonies. In 1768, British troops arrived in Boston to keep order.

The people of Boston were angry about the troops. Children called the redcoated soldiers "lobster backs." They threw rotten fruit, dirt clods, and eggs at them. Fist fights broke out between soldiers and citizens.

On the night of March 5, 1770, a large crowd of angry citizens began throwing rocks, snowballs, and sticks at a small group of soldiers. The frightened soldiers opened fire.

This 1976 U.S. postage stamp, issued for America's bicentennial celebration, shows the Boston Tea Party. That historic event took place more than 200 years before.

Eleven citizens fell dead or wounded. One of the dead was **Crispus Attucks**, an African American who had been leading protests in Boston.

Boston's newspapers reported the violence in headlines that screamed, "BOSTON MASSACRE!" For years to come, the people of Boston would remember March 5 as Massacre Day.

The Boston Tea Party

After the **Boston Massacre**, British troops were removed from Boston. The Townshend Acts were repealed, except for the tax on tea. The colonists got around the tea tax by buying cheaper Dutch tea *smuggled*, or brought in illegally, from the Netherlands. Between 1770 and 1773, the colonies were peaceful.

Then, in 1773, Parliament passed the **Tea Act**. That Act actually lowered the tea tax and made British tea less expensive. But it also let just one British company control the sale of all tea in the colonies. That angered colonial tea merchants, who would be driven out of business by the law.

The colonists began to protest again. When ships carrying British tea arrived in colonial ports, colonists refused to unload them.

In December 1773, three tea ships arrived in Boston. On the night of December 16, colonists dressed as Indians raided the ships. They smashed tea chests and dumped tea overboard. Their protest became known as the **Boston Tea Party**.

Many colonists approved of protests such as the Boston Tea Party. But the British government was furious.

Looking Back

1. Why did Parliament pass laws such as the Sugar Act and the Stamp Act?
2. What did the colonists mean when they said "no taxation without representation"?
3. How did colonists protest against laws they did not like?
4. How do people protest these days when the government does something they do not like?

Colonies Declare Independence

When news of the Boston Tea Party reached England, angry British leaders acted. Early in 1774, Parliament passed a series of new laws. Those laws were meant to punish Boston.

One law closed Boston harbor. Most of Boston's food arrived by ship. By closing the harbor, Britain hoped to starve the city into accepting British rule.

Other laws closed the Massachusetts legislature and made town meetings illegal. Courts were closed. The British military was put in charge of the colony, and a British general was named governor.

The Intolerable Acts

In America, the new laws were called the "**Intolerable Acts**." By using that name, the colonists were saying they would never *tolerate*, or accept, such laws.

The British hoped their new laws would teach all the colonies a lesson. Instead, the laws helped unite the colonies against Britain. The colonists formed groups called **Committees of Correspondence**. They wrote letters and pamphlets attacking the Acts. They spread the news about the Intolerable Acts throughout the colonies.

Soon, other colonies were helping Boston. Food arrived from faraway Virginia and South Carolina. New Hampshire sent cattle and sheep. Boston did not starve.

The First Continental Congress

In September 1774, leaders from 12 colonies met to talk about the Intolerable Acts. The meeting was called the **First Continental Congress**. It was held in Philadelphia, Pennsylvania.

Members of the Congress asked colonists to cut off all trade with Britain until the Intolerable Acts were repealed.

They asked colonists to refuse to pay British taxes. And they told colonists to prepare for war. The members agreed to meet again the following spring.

Lexington and Concord

In New England, towns and villages immediately organized militias. The Massachusetts militia called themselves **minutemen**—they were ready to fight at a minute's notice. Women and children helped also. They hid weapons, bullets, and gunpowder in bedrooms and barns.

General **Thomas Gage** was the commander of British troops in America. He was also the military governor of Massachusetts. To General Gage, it looked as if the colonists were preparing for war. In the spring of 1775, Gage learned that cannons and muskets were being hidden in **Concord**. Concord was a village near Boston. Gage decided to send troops to Concord to find those weapons. On the night of April 18, 700 British troops left Boston for Concord.

But Gage's surprise raid failed. Colonial leaders had learned of his plans. Two colonists rode through the night, warning villages along the road to Concord that the British were coming. The riders were **Paul Revere** and **William Dawes.** When General Gage reached the village of **Lexington**, 70 minutemen were waiting. After a brief fight, eight colonists lay dead.

Gage's troops marched on to Concord. In Concord, about 400 armed and angry colonists were waiting. After another brief fight, the British began to retreat.

The march back to Boston was difficult for the British. All along the road, minutemen waited, hidden behind trees and stone walls. The minutemen shot the British as they passed by. By the time the British reached Boston, 273 of them were dead or wounded.

The Second Continental Congress

In May 1775, colonial leaders met again in Philadelphia. That meeting was called the **Second Continental Congress**. The colonies and Great Britain were now at war. The colonists were determined to get their rights back. George Washington was chosen to organize and lead a colonial army. That army was called the **Continental Army**.

Some members of Congress called for *independence*. But that idea frightened many Americans. They still felt loyal to Britain and its king, **George III**. And they liked being part of Britain. They knew Britain was powerful and could protect the colonies.

Then, in January 1776, an important pamphlet appeared in the colonies. The pamphlet was called *Common Sense*. It was written by **Thomas Paine**. Paine told Americans that they had little to fear from independence. Paine asked Americans this question: ''Is it in the interest of a man to be a boy all his life?'' What do you think Paine meant by those words?

Those words convinced many Americans that independence was best for the colonies.

The Declaration of Independence

In the spring of 1776, the Second Continental Congress asked a group of its members to write a *document*, or official paper, announcing America's independence. **Thomas Jefferson** was a lawyer from Virginia. He was also a talented writer. Jefferson wrote most of the document, which became known as the **Declaration of Independence**.

The Declaration began by saying that all people are born with certain God-given rights. Those rights include the right to ''life, liberty, and the pursuit of happiness.'' The Declaration said that people set up governments to protect those

Library of Congress

The signing of the Declaration of Independence is shown often by artists. The painting of this scene hangs in the Capitol Building in Washington, D.C.

rights. If a government does not protect people's rights, people have the right to throw out that government and form a new one.

The Declaration ended by saying that ''these United Colonies are, and of right ought to be FREE AND INDEPENDENT STATES.'' From that day on, those states would be called the **United States of America**.

On July 4, 1776, Congress approved the Declaration. A new nation was born.

Looking Back
1. What were the Intolerable Acts? How did the colonies protest against them?
2. Why did General Gage decide to send troops to Concord?
3. Why did some colonists fear independence?
4. What did the Declaration of Independence say governments are for? When do people have the right to throw out a government?
5. Why do Americans today celebrate on July 4?

Chapter 4

Review

Facts First

Complete each sentence by choosing the correct ending.

1. By 1754, colonists in the British colonies
   a. did not have the same rights as people in Britain.
   b. were used to governing themselves.
   c. could elect members to Parliament.
2. After the French and Indian War, Britain
   a. gave the colonies independence.
   b. lowered the colonists' taxes.
   c. passed laws to tax the colonists.
3. The colonists thought laws for the colonies
   a. should be passed in their legislatures.
   b. should be passed by the English Parliament.
   c. should be made by the king.
4. The Stamp Act was a law that
   a. created post offices in America.
   b. taxed the colonists.
   c. was passed by the colonists.
5. When colonists said ''no taxation without representation,'' they meant
   a. colonial legislatures could not tax them.
   b. Parliament could not tax them.
   c. only the king could tax them.
6. The Intolerable Acts were laws that
   a. stopped all protest in the colonies.
   b. punished Boston by taking away rights.
   c. were passed by the Boston legislature.
7. Thomas Paine wrote *Common Sense* to
   a. stop Americans from protesting.
   b. support the idea of independence.
   c. keep colonists loyal to Britain.
8. The Declaration of Independence said the colonies
   a. were now part of Spain.
   b. would obey Parliament's laws.
   c. were now independent states.

Word Check

Write the meaning of each word below. Then use each word in a sentence.

boycott   **militia**
independence   **repeal**

Skill Builder

Find out in what years these events happened. Then write them in order.
- Britain wins the French and Indian War.
- Colonists protest taxes with the Boston Tea Party.
- The First Continental Congress meets to discuss the Intolerable Acts.
- The Second Continental Congress meets and organizes the Continental Army.
- Parliament passes the Tea Act to raise money.
- The battle at Lexington starts the war.
- The Declaration of Independence is written.

Chapter 4 Notes

Read over the chapter. Find answers to these questions:
1. What were the three parts of each colonial government?
2. Why were colonists angry about new taxes and laws forced on them by the British after the French and Indian War?
3. How did the colonists protest against those laws?
4. What did colonial leaders decide to do at the First Continental Congress?
5. What happened at the Second Continental Congress?

Be a Historian

Find out about someone who is making a protest against a government in our own time. Make an oral report on that protest.

Chapter 5 **The War for Independence (1776-1783)**

A British officer in the Revolutionary War painted this picture. It shows the British attacking Fort Lee, New Jersey, which is on the Hudson River.

The United States declared its independence from Great Britain in July of 1776. But winning independence proved to be very difficult. Great Britain was the wealthiest and most powerful nation in the world. And Britain was determined to keep its colonies in America.

It would take eight years for the United States to win the War for Independence.

- How were the colonies able to win the war against the most powerful nation in the world?
- Who sided with the British and who helped the patriots during the war?
- What did the United States gain in the treaty that ended the war?

Key Words   You will be using these words in this chapter. Look them up in the glossary at the back of Part 1.

alliance	**treaty**
rebellion	**volunteer**

Britain's Strengths and Problems

In 1775, Great Britain was the strongest military power in the world. Its army in America was much larger than the Continental Army. Its navy had more ships than the Americans had. British soldiers were highly trained and experienced in battle. British ships could bring troops and supplies to America and move troops from place to place.

Britain was also the wealthiest nation in the world. It could buy the weapons and ammunition needed to fight the war.

Britain's Problems

But the British faced some serious problems in fighting the war. The first problem was the distance between the two countries. America was 3000 miles away, and it took weeks for British ships to reach America. British commanders sometimes had to hold off an attack until new troops arrived from Britain. The commanders also received their orders from the government in Britain. Those orders were often out-of-date by the time they reached America.

A second problem was America's size. America was huge. The British were fighting in a country that was 1000 miles long and 600 miles wide.

A third problem was getting soldiers for the British army. Britain needed more troops than it had to defeat the colonies. So, the government hired 30,000 **Hessian** soldiers to fight. (Hessians are Germans.)

Looking Back
1. In what ways was Britain stronger than the colonies at the start of the war?
2. What were Britain's problems in fighting the war?

America's Weak Position

The new United States was not prepared to go to war. For one thing, not all Americans wanted to break from Britain. Most Americans supported the war and independence. But about a third of all Americans were *against* the war. They remained loyal to Britain. The Americans who wanted independence were called **patriots**. The Americans who did not want independence were called **loyalists**.

Continental Congress Has Little Power

The Americans also had other serious problems. The Continental Congress was now running the new country. But it had little power. It could not collect taxes. It could only *ask* the states for money, and the states never sent enough. So, the Continental Army was always short of funds for weapons, food, clothing, and other supplies.

A Small Untrained Army

The Continental Army was much smaller than the British army. Most of its soldiers were *volunteers*. The volunteers often refused to sign up for more than a year. Just when they had learned to fight, they went home. So, the army was always short of troops.

Colonial soldiers had little discipline. Many of them obeyed the orders they liked and disobeyed orders they did not agree with. Soldiers from one state sometimes refused to fight alongside soldiers from another state.

A New and Small Navy

When the war began, the United States had no navy. By early 1776, the Continental Navy was set up and had its first ships. But those ships were no match for Britain's many warships.

The Metropolitan Museum of Art, gift of John Stewart Kennedy, 1897. (9734)

General Washington and his troops cross the Delaware River on Christmas Day, 1776. This famous scene was painted in 1851. The painting by Emanuel Leutze (1816–1868) hangs in the Metropolitan Museum of Art, New York City.

Overcoming the Weakness

The new United States had strong leaders. The leaders kept the colonists together. One of the most important leaders was George Washington. Under his leadership, the Continental Army became a daring fighting force. Other important leaders were patriots such as John and Samuel Adams, John Hancock, Patrick Henry, Thomas Jefferson, and Benjamin Franklin. They wrote articles and gave speeches that convinced Americans to support the war. They also helped run the new country.

Americans proved to be courageous fighters. They learned to fight differently from European troops. The British and Hessian troops wore bright uniforms. They marched out in the open, and they fought in neat rows. But the Americans wore clothing that blended with the woods. They hid behind trees to fire at their enemy. That kind of fighting surprised and confused the British.

Looking Back

1. How was the United States weak at the start of the war?
2. What strengths did the United States have?
3. Imagine it is 1776. Someone asks whether you think Britain or the United States will win the war. How will you answer? Why?

The War Begins

Most of the fighting early in the war took place in New England and the middle colonies.

In June 1775, two months after the battle at Concord, British and American troops fought in the hills surrounding Boston. That battle was called the **Battle of Bunker Hill**. The British won that battle, but they paid a high price: 1000 British troops were killed or wounded.

After the Battle of Bunker Hill, the British camped in Boston, awaiting new troops and supplies. In March 1776, General Washington put cannons on a hill overlooking Boston. The British realized they could not hold the city. So they left Boston and sailed to Canada.

The British Take New York City

Washington then marched his army south to New York City. In August, 32,000 British and Hessian troops arrived in New York. Washington and his army were forced to retreat. They traveled across New Jersey and then crossed the Delaware River into Pennsylvania.

After the defeat in New York, many of Washington's troops *deserted*, or ran away. By December of 1776, the Continental Army had shrunk to only a few thousand troops. Defeat seemed near. In a letter to his brother, Washington wrote: "I think the game is pretty near up."

The Americans Win at Trenton

On Christmas Day, 1776, Washington's troops were camped near the Delaware River in Pennsylvania. It was a freezing winter day. Snow and ice were on the ground and in the river. Across the river, in New Jersey, Hessian soldiers were celebrating the holiday in the town of Trenton.

That night, Washington and his troops crossed the river in small boats. The Hessians were completely surprised. After a short battle, they surrendered. Washington's troops captured about a thousand prisoners.

Washington's victory at Trenton was an important one. The victory raised the *morale*, or confidence, of the troops. And news of the victory brought thousands of volunteers into the Continental Army.

The British Develop a Plan for Victory

The British came up with a plan to win the war in 1777. Their plan was to capture the state of New York and cut off New England from the rest of the colonies. Men and supplies from the other colonies then would not be able to get into New England. And the ***rebellion*** would end.

To carry out the plan, General **William Howe** would march north up the Hudson River Valley to Albany, New York. At the same time, General **John Burgoyne** would march south into New York from Canada. The two armies would meet in Albany. British forces would then control the entire Hudson River Valley.

The American Capital Is Taken

In the summer of 1777, General Howe was supposed to put the plan into action. But he decided first to attack Philadelphia in Pennsylvania. Philadelphia was the new capital of the United States. Howe's troops marched on Philadelphia. Washington tried to stop them but failed. On September 26, Howe captured Philadelphia.

Looking Back
1. Where did most of the fighting take place early in the war?
2. How did General Washington's victory over the Hessians at Trenton make the Continental Army stronger?

WAR FOR INDEPENDENCE

① **Boston, MA**
② **Lexington, MA**
③ **New York, NY**
④ **Fort Ticonderoga, NY**
⑤ **Saratoga, NY**
⑥ **Philadelphia, PA**
⑦ **Valley Forge, PA**
⑧ **Yorktown, VA**
⑨ **Cowpens, SC**

The Turning Point

After the British took Philadelphia, General Washington retreated to **Valley Forge** in Pennsylvania. There he and the Continental Army set up winter camp. That winter was more terrible than battle. Washington's troops lacked food, blankets, and clothing. Their feet and legs froze. Hundreds of men died from diseases. Thousands of others deserted.

But Washington used the months at Valley Forge to prepare his men for the fighting ahead. A tough officer from Germany, **Baron von Steuben**, trained the Americans. He spent the winter teaching them how to drill and fight like professional soldiers.

The British March from Canada

While General Howe was moving north in 1777, General Burgoyne was moving south. He began his part of the British plan for victory by marching from Canada into New York. On July 6, 1777, his troops captured Fort Ticonderoga in New York. They then began marching toward Albany.

But the British plan began to fail. General Burgoyne's troops could not move quickly. The army traveled with many extra people. Indians, loyalists, and a wagon train of soldiers' wives and children followed the troops. There were also hundreds of heavy wagons carrying supplies and cannons. Day after day, troops had to hack out roads for the wagons through woods and swamps.

During their slow march, the British were constantly attacked by patriots who appeared suddenly, then disappeared. When the British finally reached the Hudson River, their food was gone. They could not find food nearby because patriots had burned cornfields for miles around.

The Turning Point at Saratoga

In October, Burgoyne's troops approached **Saratoga**, a town near Albany. There they waited for supplies from General Howe. But militias of patriots from New England and New York began attacking them. About 17,000 patriots altogether surrounded Burgoyne's army. Outnumbered, the British surrendered on October 17, 1777.

Saratoga was an important victory for the Americans. It showed Europe that Americans could win over the British. France decided to help the Americans. In 1778, France formed an ***alliance*** with the United States and began sending money, supplies, and military officers to America.

Also, in 1778, Washington's troops completed their training at Valley Forge. They were toughened and ready for battle.

Looking Back
1. How did Washington use the winter months at Valley Forge?
2. Why was the victory at Saratoga important for the Americans?
3. If you had been with Washington at Valley Forge, would you have stayed with the army? Why or why not?

The Road to Victory: 1778-1783

In June 1778, a new British general took charge of British forces in America. His name was **Sir Henry Clinton**. General Clinton pulled the British troops out of Philadelphia and marched them toward New York City.

General Washington followed the British across New Jersey and fought them. But the Americans could not stop them. The British reached New York in July.

The Battle Moves to the South

General Clinton then came up with a new plan: He would attack the Americans in the South. Clinton left an army in New York to hold New York City. He sailed south with another army. The last battles of the war would be fought in the southern colonies.

In 1779 and 1780, British troops under Clinton and General **Charles Cornwallis** won several victories in Georgia, North Carolina, and South Carolina. Many patriots became discouraged. But others kept up the fight against the British.

Throughout the South, small *guerrilla* groups fought the British. (A guerrilla is a fighter who is not part of the regular army.) Guerrilla groups made quick hit-and-run raids on the British: They killed British troops and destroyed supplies. They freed American prisoners. Then they disappeared into southern swamps and forests.

In January 1781, the Americans finally won a major victory over British forces at Cowpens, South Carolina. General Cornwallis moved north to Virginia. The British camped near **Yorktown**, a village on the Chesapeake Bay.

Victory at Yorktown

In New York, General Washington received news of the British move to Virginia. With the help of the French, Washington planned a trap for the British army at Yorktown.

Washington made it look as if he were preparing to attack British troops in New York City. But he secretly moved most of his army south to Virginia. At the same time, French warships sailed into Chesapeake Bay.

In September, Washington's army surrounded Yorktown. French ships blocked Chesapeake Bay so that Cornwallis could not escape by sea. Cornwallis held on for three weeks. Then, on October 19, 1781, he surrendered.

The battle at Yorktown was the last major battle of the war. The defeat of Cornwallis convinced the British to accept American independence.

Peace

On September 3, 1783, Great Britain and the United States signed a *treaty* ending the war. That treaty was called the **Treaty of Paris**.

In the Treaty of Paris, Britain accepted the United States as an independent nation. The treaty also described the size of the new nation: The United States stretched from the Great Lakes south to Florida and from the Atlantic coast west to the Mississippi River. Britain still controlled Canada.

After eight years of struggle, the United States had won its independence.

Looking Back

1. How did the Americans and French trap the British at Yorktown?
2. What did the Americans gain in the Treaty of Paris?

These U.S. postage stamps are part of a special series that was issued in 1976. The stamps honor people who helped win the War for Independence.

Fighting for Their Country

The colonists had fought a difficult war to keep their rights. But not every American had those rights. As you read, women did not have many of the rights given to men. And most African Americans in America were slaves; they had none of the rights that white Americans had. Still, many Americans who had few rights fought for the country's right to be free.

Women in the War

Many American women went with their husbands into the army. They helped set up and keep camp and acted as nurses for soldiers who were sick or wounded. When the army marched, women helped carry food and supplies.

Some women also fought in battle. One of those women was **Deborah Sampson**. She fought as a regular soldier in the Continental Army for over a year, disguised as a man. During that year, she fought in many battles and was wounded twice. After the war, she was granted a full soldier's *pension*, or payment for service, by Congress.

African American Patriots

African Americans also helped the United States win its independence. At least 5000 African Americans took part in the fighting, from Lexington to Yorktown.

Oliver Cromwell was a free African American. He joined Washington's army, fought with Washington at Trenton, and was with him at Valley Forge. Cromwell was still fighting with Washington when the war ended.

After the war, some people asked this question: If African Americans are willing to fight and die for the freedom of America, shouldn't they enjoy that freedom too? Many answered *yes*. Pennsylvania and the New England states passed laws ending slavery. In other states, slaves who had served their country were freed.

Looking Back

1. How did women help the United States win its independence?
2. Why did some Americans turn against slavery during the war?

Chapter 5

Review

Facts First
Use words below to complete each sentence.

Britain	**patriots**
France	**Philadelphia**
loyalists	**Saratoga**
Mississippi River	**treaty**

1. _____ was the most powerful nation in the world in 1776.
2. Americans who wanted independence were _____.
3. Americans who did not want to break away from Britain were _____.
4. The capital of the United States in 1777 was _____.
5. The victory at _____ showed everyone that the patriots could win against Britain.
6. _____ formed an alliance with the United States.
7. The U.S. victory at Yorktown convinced the British to sign a _____ to end the war.
8. After the Treaty of Paris, the U.S. controlled land west to the _____.

Word Check
Write the meaning of each of these words. Then use each word in a sentence.

alliance	**treaty**
rebellion	**volunteer**

Skill Builder
The Declaration of Independence declared the 13 colonies free and independent states. They became the first 13 of the United States. Make a map of the first 13 states.

Chapter 5 Notes
Read over the chapter. Find answers to these questions:
1. What strengths and problems did Britain have in beginning the war against the Americans?
2. What problems and strengths did the Americans have?
3. How did the British plan to defeat the Americans in 1777?
4. Why was Saratoga an important victory for the Americans?
5. What territories did the British give up in the Treaty of Paris? What did they keep control of?

Be a Historian
Today, people are fighting for freedom in other places in the world. Find out about one of those places. Read newspapers and magazines. Watch and listen to the news on television and radio. Then report what you learned.

Bonus
Each of the people below helped America win its independence. Find out about one of these people. Then report what you learned.

Abigail Adams	John Paul Jones
Samuel Adams	Marquis de Lafayette
Crispus Attucks	Thomas Paine
Nathan Hale	Molly Pitcher
Patrick Henry	

Unit 2

Review

What Do You Know?
Complete each sentence by choosing the correct ending.
1. In America, British colonists
   a. set up their own governments.
   b. had no self-government.
   c. had no individual rights.
2. After the French and Indian War, Britain
   a. let the colonists settle anywhere.
   b. removed its troops from America.
   c. taxed the colonists.
3. Colonists said Parliament could not tax them because colonists
   a. were not British citizens.
   b. had no one to speak for them in Parliament.
   c. were too poor to pay taxes.
4. After the Boston Tea Party, Britain
   a. stopped taxing the colonists.
   b. tried to punish the colonies.
   c. gave the colonies their freedom.
5. The Declaration of Independence said the colonies were now
   a. free and independent states.
   b. part of New France.
   c. ready to obey all British laws.
6. The United States began the War for Independence
   a. with a larger army than the British.
   b. with Hessian soldiers on its side.
   c. with little money and a small army.
7. An American strength in the war was
   a. the Continental Navy.
   b. the support of the loyalists.
   c. their new style of fighting.
8. In the Treaty of Paris, Britain
   a. accepted the U.S. as an independent nation.
   b. gave Canada to the United States.
   c. said America would never be free.

What Do You Think?
The Declaration of Independence states that all people have the right to "life, liberty, and the pursuit of happiness." What do you think those words mean?

Skill Builder
Find each place below on a map of the United States. Then write a short report telling why each place was important during the War for Independence.
Lexington, Massachusetts
Philadelphia, Pennsylvania
Saratoga, New York
Valley Forge, Pennsylvania
Yorktown, Virginia

Unit 2 Notes
Look over the unit to find answers to these questions:
1. Why did the colonies become unhappy about being ruled by Britain?
2. In what ways did the colonists show Britain they were not happy with British laws?
3. What did the Declaration of Independence say?
4. Which seemed stronger at the beginning of the war in 1776—Britain or the U.S.? Why?
5. What are some reasons the U.S. won the war?
6. What did the U.S. gain from the war besides independence?

Word Builder
Write a story about the American Revolution. Use all the key words listed below.

Key Words
boycott	repeal
independence	treaty
militia	volunteer

unit 3 The New Nation

Philadelphia, Pennsylvania—July 4, 1788

Throughout the city of Philadelphia, church bells ring. In the harbor, ships fire their cannons. The biggest celebration in the city's history is under way: The nation has just approved a new Constitution!

Thousands of people line the city's streets to watch the huge July 4th parade. One of those people is Dr. Benjamin Rush. Dr. Rush was one of the leaders who signed the Declaration of Independence 12 years ago in 1776.

The parade is long and exciting: Troops on horseback and bands of musicians pass by. Then come decorated wagons pulled by horses.

Groups of Philadelphia's workers also march in the parade. Some 450 carpenters lead the way. Brickmakers, boat builders, sailmakers, carpenters, tailors, barbers, blacksmiths, and ropemakers march proudly past. Each group has its own flag and style of dress.

A large wagon passes by. It carries women who are using a new kind of machine. The machines make thread out of cotton fiber. The whirring machines amaze the people watching the parade.

Religious leaders of every faith march by together. A Jewish rabbi, a Catholic priest, and a Protestant minister walk together.

That night, as the city begins to quiet down, Dr. Rush writes a friend. "No victory in the last war brought such joy to the people as today's celebration."

Dr. Rush stops for a moment to remember the troubles of the last few years. Then he adds happily, " 'Tis done. We have become a nation."

In Our Time

In 1788, the people of the United States approved a new Constitution. The Constitution was a plan of government for the country. It also was a plan that protected the rights and freedoms of the American people.

Today, 200 years later, the Constitution is still working. The Constitution still guides our leaders. It still protects our rights and freedoms. What are those rights and freedoms? In what ways are they important to you?

1781	1786	1788	1789	1791	1794	1796	1800
Articles of Confederation ratified	Shays' Rebellion	Constitution ratified	George Washington elected President	Bill of Rights ratified	Whiskey Rebellion	John Adams elected President	Thomas Jefferson elected President

Chapter ⑥ **A Difficult Beginning**

The Liberty Bell was rung July 8, 1776, to celebrate the Declaration of Independence.

The War for Independence kept the 13 states united. But when peace came in 1783, each state wanted to go its own way.

The years from 1783 to 1787 were hard for the young nation. By 1787, many Americans were wondering if the United States could survive.

- What kind of state governments were set up after independence?
- What was the first national government like?
- What problems did the national government face?
- Why did many Americans call for changes in the national government?

Key Words   You will be using these words in this chapter. Look them up in the glossary at the back of Part 1.

      election   **national**
      limit   **representative**

Independence National Historical Park Collection

The New State Governments

When the United States declared its independence in 1776, the colonies became *states*. They turned their colonial governments into state governments. The state governments were like the colonial governments in many ways. They kept many colonial laws. Their colonial legislatures became state legislatures.

But life under British rule had taught Americans some important lessons about government. So, Americans made changes when they set up their new state governments.

Written Constitutions

Americans in each state made sure that their **state constitution** was written down. A constitution is a plan of government. Great Britain did not have a written constitution. That had caused misunderstandings between the government and the colonists. For example, nowhere was it written that Parliament had the right to tax the colonies. But Parliament taxed them anyway.

Americans wanted the rules of government and people's rights written down for all to read. In that way, there could be no mistakes about what the law said. By 1780, all 13 states had written new state constitutions.

Government of the People

Americans also made sure that each state government was a **democracy**, a government run by the people. State constitutions gave people control of their governments through *elections*. In those elections, the people in the state elected certain people to be their *representatives* to state legislatures. Those representatives acted for the people. They set taxes and made other laws for the whole state.

In a General Convention.

Begun and holden at the Capitol, in the City of Williamsburg, on Monday the sixth day of May, one thousand seven hundred and seventy six, and continued, by adjournments to the ____ day of June following.

A Constitution, or form of Government, agreed to and resolved upon by the Delegates and Representatives of the several Counties and Corporations of Virginia.

Where ___ George the Third, King of Great Britain and ___

One of the first state constitutions was written in Virginia, in 1776. It contained the first bill of rights.

Limiting Government Officials

Under the British, Americans learned that government officials sometimes *abuse* their power—use their power to do things that are wrong or harmful to people.

To protect the people from such abuses, state constitutions put **limits** on the power of government officials. The constitutions said that officials had only those powers listed in their constitution. If any official abused those powers, that official could be taken out of the government.

Protecting the People's Rights

Americans also made sure their state constitutions protected the rights of people. Most state constitutions included a **bill of rights**. A bill of rights lists the rights and freedoms that belong to people and that a government cannot take away.

The states' bills of rights often included such rights as: the right to a trial by jury, the right to worship as a person chose, the right to say or write something without fear of arrest, and the right to own property.

State constitutions also gave Americans another important right—the right to vote. But not every American had that right. In most states, only men who owned property could vote. Blacks and Native Americans could not vote in any state. And women could not vote, except in New Jersey. (New Jersey later took the right to vote away from women.)

Women's Rights Not Protected

The state constitutions did not give equal rights to everyone. Women did not have many of the rights that men had. As you read, they were not given the right to vote. They also could not run for office or serve on juries. A wife did not have the right to take her husband to court even if he mistreated her.

Women did not have the same property rights as men. A single woman could own property. But if she got married, all her property belonged to her husband. Any money she earned belonged to him. She could not buy or sell anything unless he agreed. If a couple divorced, their children belonged to the husband.

Looking Back

1. Why did Americans want written constitutions?
2. How did state constitutions give control of state governments to the people?
3. How did the state constitutions make sure government officials did not harm the people?
4. What is a bill of rights?
5. Why do you think the state constitutions were not fair to women?

The First National Government

During the War for Independence, the United States was run by the Continental Congress. The Continental Congress was made up of leaders from each state. The leaders realized that the states needed to have a **national** government—a government that ruled over all the states.

The Continental Congress wrote a constitution that set up a national government. The constitution was called the **Articles of Confederation.** In 1781, the states approved it.

The Confederation Congress

The Articles of Confederation set up a government that was run only by a congress. Members of Congress were chosen by the state legislatures. Each state had one vote in Congress.

The Articles of Confederation gave Congress some powers. It could
- make laws for the country,
- declare war and make peace,
- borrow money,
- make coins and print paper money, and
- form alliances and make treaties with other nations.

But the powers of Congress were strictly limited. For example:
- Congress could pass laws. But it did not have the power to make the states obey its laws.
- Congress did not have the power to tax people. Only the states could do that. If Congress wanted money, it had to ask the states for it.
- Congress could declare war. But it had to depend on the states to supply men and money for an army.
- Congress could not control trade with other nations or among the states.
- Congress did not have the power to end arguments between states.

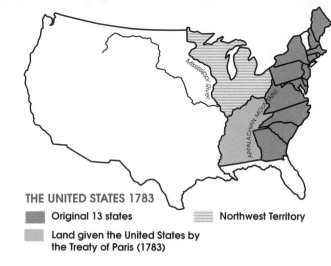

THE UNITED STATES 1783

▪ Original 13 states ▨ Northwest Territory

▨ Land given the United States by the Treaty of Paris (1783)

A Weak National Government

Congress had limited powers for a reason: Most Americans feared a strong national government. They believed that the British government had abused its powers, and they worried that a strong United States government might do the same. So, the Articles of Confederation set up a national government that was weak. The government was supposed to unite the states and hold them together. But it did not have more power than the states.

The weakness of the national government caused problems when the war ended. The national government had no courts. So, if states quarreled with each other, the national government could not end the argument. Without a national court system, Congress could not make anyone obey its laws. If a state did not like a law passed by Congress, it simply ignored it.

When Congress asked for money, many states refused to send it. So, Congress never had the money it needed to pay the nation's war debts and run the country.

Looking Back

1. What were the Articles of Confederation?
2. What powers did the Articles of Confederation give to Congress?
3. What important powers were not given to Congress?
4. Why did Americans fear a strong national government in 1781?

The Western Territories

After the war, in 1783, the United States and Britain signed a peace treaty — the Treaty of Paris. The treaty gave the United States the land between the Appalachian Mountains and the Mississippi River. The northern half of this area was called the **Northwest Territory**.

The Land Ordinance of 1785

Americans began moving into the territory. To make their claims, they simply walked into the wilderness and settled on the land they wanted. They did not clearly mark the land to show what areas they claimed, so settlers often argued over land claims.

In 1785, Congress came up with a plan to end such arguments. That plan was the **Land Ordinance of 1785**. Under that plan, government surveyors carefully measured the land. Then they divided it into parts. They wrote a record of the parts. Now when a settler bought a part, there could be no argument about property lines.

The Northwest Ordinance of 1787

With people settling in the Northwest Territory, Congress faced new questions: How should the territory be governed? How would the territory become new states?

Congress passed a law called the **Northwest Ordinance of 1787**. That law set up a plan for governing the Northwest Territory.

The Northwest Ordinance divided the Northwest Territory into several smaller territories. Congress sent a governor to run each new territory. When there were 5000 people in a territory, those people could elect a legislature. When there were 60,000 people in a territory, the legislature could apply to Congress to become a state.

Settlers in the Northwest Territory had the same rights as other Americans. But slavery was not allowed there.

The Northwest Ordinance worked well. It set up a plan that allowed the new nation to grow.

Problems with Britain and Spain

After the War for Independence, Britain promised to withdraw British troops from the United States. But Britain kept troops in forts throughout the Northwest Territory to protect the British fur trade. American settlers were angry when they found British troops still on American soil.

American settlers also had problems with Spain. Both Spain and the United States claimed the same land near the Gulf of Mexico. Spain also controlled the Mississippi River near the Gulf of Mexico. To stop Americans from settling in the area, the Spanish closed the river to American boats. That meant farmers in the West could not use the river to ship their grain to customers.

Congress was furious over the actions of the British and Spanish in the West. It protested to the governments of both nations. But neither government paid any attention. Britain and Spain knew that Congress could not raise an army to back up its protests.

Looking Back

1. What land was given to the United States in the Treaty of Paris?
2. What was the Northwest Ordinance? How did it help the United States grow?
3. Why did Spain close the Mississippi River to Americans?
4. *Map work*: Look at a large map of the United States today. Point out the states that developed from the Northwest Territory.

During Shays' Rebellion angry farmers protested against high taxes in Massachusetts in 1786.

Troubled Times

The years from 1783 to 1787 were full of problems for the young nation. Most members of Congress were more loyal to their states than to the national government. Sometimes, they did not even show up for meetings of Congress.

The country was also in a *depression*. A depression is a time when many businesses lose money or fail and many people are out of work. Many Americans had little money. Congress also had little money.

States Quarrel with Each Other

The 13 states did not cooperate with Congress or with each other. States quarreled over land. They quarreled over trade between states. States often taxed the goods of other states. For example, New York taxed firewood from Connecticut and cabbages from New Jersey. Connecticut and New Jersey, in turn, taxed goods from New York.

States also quarreled about money. Most states printed their own paper money and they refused to accept the money of other states. Soon, there were so many different kinds of money floating around that paper money became nearly worthless.

Congress did not have the power to force the states to work together.

Shays' Rebellion

The depression of the 1780s was hard on farmers. In good times, many farmers had borrowed money to buy land. Then crop prices dropped, and farmers could not make any money. Many farmers could not pay their debts or taxes. The courts ordered their farms sold. Those who still could not pay were sometimes sent to jail.

Farmers in Massachusetts asked their legislature to help them. They asked for lower taxes. But the legislature did nothing. In 1786, farmers, led by a Revolutionary War veteran named **Daniel Shays,** rebelled. Mobs of angry farmers surrounded the courthouses to keep courts from opening. They hoped to stop judges from ordering farms sold and sending farmers to jail.

Massachusetts asked Congress to help put down the rebellion. But Congress had no army to send. The Massachusetts militia finally ended **Shays' Rebellion**.

A Call for Change

Shays' Rebellion frightened many Americans. It showed that the national government was too weak to protect Americans from rebels.

George Washington and other leaders became convinced that the nation could not survive under its present government. They asked for a meeting of all the states. In 1787, 55 Americans met in Philadelphia to talk about changing the Articles of Confederation. They came from all the states except Rhode Island.

Looking Back

1. Why were the years from 1783 to 1787 hard times for many Americans?
2. What did the states quarrel about?
3. Why didn't Congress stop the quarrels?
4. Why did some Americans call for changes in the national government?

Chapter 6

Review

Facts First

Complete each sentence by choosing the correct ending.

1. In 1776, the states set up state governments
   a. that gave power to the people.
   b. that were run by a king.
   c. with no legislatures.

2. State constitutions
   a. were not written.
   b. put limits on government powers.
   c. usually had no bill of rights.

3. In most states, the right to vote was given to
   a. men with property.
   b. women with property.
   c. Blacks and Native Americans.

4. The Confederation Congress
   a. ran the country well.
   b. had the respect of other nations.
   c. was too weak to govern the nation.

5. The Northwest Ordinance was a plan that helped
   a. slavery spread west.
   b. organize territories into states.
   c. give land back to the British.

6. Under the Articles of Confederation, the states
   a. worked well together.
   b. quarreled over taxes and trade.
   c. cooperated with Congress.

7. During Shays' Rebellion, farmers
   a. surrounded courts to keep them closed.
   b. held a parade to celebrate low taxes.
   c. fought against the British.

8. After Shays' Rebellion, government leaders
   a. took over Massachusetts courts.
   b. called for a stronger national government.
   c. asked the British to take over again.

Word Check

Write the meaning of each of these words. Then use each word in a sentence.

election   national
limit   representative

Skill Builder

Look at a map of the United States. Use it to answer these questions:

1. In what part of the United States were the first 13 states? (eastern, middle, or western)
2. What is the name of your state?
3. In what part of the country is your state? (eastern, middle, or western)
4. Was your state one of the United States in 1781?
5. Find Ohio and Oregon on the map. Which one do you think joined the United States first? Why do you say that?

Chapter 6 Notes

Read over the chapter. Find answers to these questions:

1. What were the Articles of Confederation?
2. What powers did the Confederation Congress have?
3. What powers did the Confederation Congress not have?
4. Why did the states set up a weak national government?
5. What did the Northwest Ordinance of 1787 do?

Be a Historian

Find out more about your state's history. Answer these questions:

1. When did your state become a state?
2. When was the state constitution written?
3. Where was the first state capital?
4. Who were some early state leaders?

Chapter 7 The Constitution of the United States

This engraving shows Philadelphia's Independence Hall at the time of the Constitutional Convention.

During the hot summer of 1787, delegates from the states held a meeting in Philadelphia. For over four months, they met in a place called Independence Hall. That meeting came to be known as the *Constitutional Convention.*

The delegates came to Philadelphia to change the Articles of Confederation. But they did much more than that. They wrote a whole new plan of government for the nation. They called that plan the *Constitution of the United States.*

- Who were the delegates to the Constitutional Convention?
- What compromises did the delegates make while writing the Constitution?
- How was the new national government organized?
- How did the Constitution limit the power of the nation's government?

Key Words   You will be using these words in this chapter. Look them up in the glossary at the back of Part 1.

compromise	**federal**
delegate	**ratify**

The Constitutional Convention

In May 1787, **delegates** from 12 states arrived in Philadelphia for a *convention,* or meeting. They came to the meeting to discuss the Articles of Confederation and to make changes that would improve the government. Each delegate had been chosen by his state legislature. Only one state, Rhode Island, sent no delegates. The people of Rhode Island did not want the Articles of Confederation changed.

The delegates who came to Philadelphia believed that the Articles of Confederation *had* to be changed. The new nation was in trouble. It was not strong and united under the Articles of Confederation.

The Delegates

The delegates were well qualified for the job of planning a new government.

More than half of the 55 delegates had served in the Continental Congress. Many of the delegates were lawyers. Many had helped to write their state constitutions. And most of them had served in their state legislatures. Because they were leaders in their state governments, they understood how a government should work.

George Washington— Constitutional Convention President

The first action of the delegates was to elect a president of the convention. They chose George Washington. No man was more respected than he.

As president, Washington's job was to keep the convention running smoothly— not an easy job. The delegates often disagreed. Sometimes they shouted angrily at each other. Sometimes angry delegates threatened to walk out of the convention. But Washington's calm leadership kept the convention together through the summer.

This scene shows the Constitutional Convention delegates at work. In the background James Madison of Virginia takes careful notes.

James Madison — Father of the Constitution

James Madison of Virginia was the best-prepared delegate at the convention. He had read everything he could about government. He came to Philadelphia with strong ideas about the United States government.

James Madison believed that the Articles of Confederation should be set aside. He thought they should be replaced by a completely new constitution.

From the start of the convention, Madison worked hard to convince other delegates that they should write a new constitution. He had many ideas about how the new government should be organized and how to keep any person or group from becoming too powerful. Because so many of his ideas were put into the Constitution, Madison is known as the *Father of the Constitution.*

During the convention, Madison took notes on every speech. He wrote down everything the delegates discussed and voted on. From his notes, we know what happened each day of the convention.

Benjamin Franklin Helps Keep the Delegates Together

Benjamin Franklin of Pennsylvania was the oldest delegate. He was 81 years old. In his long life, Franklin had been a successful printer, writer, scientist, and inventor. He was a popular and respected man throughout the United States.

Franklin had helped Thomas Jefferson write the Declaration of Independence. During the War for Independence, he had served as the United States' representative to France. And in 1783, he had helped to write the peace treaty that ended the war.

Now in his last years, Benjamin Franklin was still able to help his country. Delegates at the convention came to him for advice. He helped end many bitter arguments. His sense of humor cooled hot tempers.

Looking Back
1. What was George Washington's role at the convention?
2. Why is James Madison called the Father of the Constitution?
3. What role did Benjamin Franklin play at the convention?

A Constitution of Compromises

The delegates at the Constitutional Convention agreed that the nation needed a new government. But they disagreed about what that government should be like. In fact, they sometimes disagreed so strongly that the convention nearly came to an early end.

The Virginia Plan

Early in the convention, Edmund Randolph of Virginia presented a plan for a new national government. The plan had been written by James Madison and the other Virginia delegates. That plan became known as the **Virginia Plan**.

The Virginia Plan called for a national government with three parts, or *branches*. The first branch was the **legislative branch**. It would be made up of Congress.

The second branch was the **executive branch**. It would be headed by a president.

The third branch was the **judicial branch**. It would be made up of the nation's courts.

The Debate over Representation

Most delegates agreed that the new government should have three branches. But they disagreed with other ideas in the Virginia Plan. The biggest disagreement was about **representation** in Congress—how many representatives each state could send to Congress.

The Virginia Plan said that representation should be based on *population*, or the number of people who lived in a state. States with more people would have more representatives—and votes—in Congress. Larger states supported that idea.

But delegates from small states disagreed. They said the Virginia Plan gave large states too much power.

After two weeks of heated discussion, delegates from the small states came up with a plan of their own. It was called the **New Jersey Plan**. The New Jersey Plan called for three branches, like the Virginia Plan. But the New Jersey Plan gave each state the same number of votes in Congress.

For a month, delegates from large and small states argued about the two plans. They could not reach an agreement. Some delegates began to fear that the convention would break down over the question of representation.

The Great Compromise

Benjamin Franklin realized that only a *compromise* could save the convention. In a compromise, people give up the ideas they cannot agree on. They find ideas they all can agree on.

Franklin helped the delegates from Connecticut write a plan that both large and small states could accept. That plan is known as the **Great Compromise**.

The Great Compromise called for a Congress that was made up of two parts or *houses*. The first part would be the **House of Representatives**. The second would be the **Senate**.

Representation in the House of Representatives would be based on population. Larger states would send more representatives than smaller states.

Representation in the Senate would be the same for all states. Each state would send two senators to the Senate.

Looking Back
1. What did small states dislike about the Virginia Plan?
2. How did the Great Compromise solve the problem of representation?

The Great Seal of the United States stands for the American government. It was adopted by the U.S. government in 1782. This picture shows an early Great Seal. Everything in the design has a special meaning. For example, the 13 arrows stand for the 13 colonies and their fight for freedom.

Library of Congress

Other Compromises

During the debate over the Great Compromise, another important question was raised: Should slaves be counted as part of a state's population when deciding representation? Northern delegates said *no*. They argued that slaves were property. So, slaves should not be counted as people in a state.

Southerners wanted slaves to be counted as people. That way, the southern states would have more representatives in Congress.

Finally, the convention agreed that only three-fifths of the slaves in a state would be counted as part of the population. That agreement was called the **Three-Fifths Rule**.

The Slave Trade

The delegates also reached an agreement on the slave trade. Most northern delegates wanted to end the slave trade. That would mean that no new slaves could be brought into the United States from other countries.

But southern delegates wanted the slave trade to continue. Southern planters wanted slaves to work their plantations.

After angry debates, the delegates reached a compromise. Both sides agreed that the slave trade would continue for 20 more years. Then, in 1808, Congress could vote to end it.

Trade Between States and Other Countries

Another bitter argument had to do with the trade of all kinds of goods. Many delegates wanted the national government to control trade between states. They also wanted the national government to control trade with other countries. But that idea worried some southerners.

Planters in the South lived by raising crops that they sold to other countries. They did not want the government to tax *exports*, or products sent out of the country for sale.

Again, the delegates reached a compromise. The national government would have the power to control trade between states and with other countries. But the national government could not tax exports.

Looking Back

1. What compromise did the delegates reach on the slave trade?
2. What agreement did the delegates reach on the question of trade between states? between states and other countries?
3. Why should government leaders be willing to compromise?

The New Plan of Government

After months of discussion, the delegates finished their work. They had not changed the Articles of Confederation. Instead, they had written an entirely new plan of government for the United States. Committees then worked on the plan to make sure every word was right. On September 17, 1787, the delegates signed the new plan—the **Constitution of the United States**. It was now ready to show to the American people.

"We the People of the United States"

The Constitution begins with a *preamble*, or introduction, that says the Constitution is set up and put in place by the people of the United States. It then tells what the Constitution will do for the American people. The Constitution will
- unite the states into a strong nation.
- set up *fair* laws for *all* Americans.
- set up a government that can keep peace within the nation.
- set up a government that can protect the nation from enemies.
- set up a government that can help all Americans lead better lives.
- make sure the government remains strong so that future Americans can enjoy the "blessings of liberty."

The Constitution Sets Up a Republic

The Constitution created a government for a **republic**. In a republic, the people elect many kinds of representatives to run the government for them.

The Constitution says what kinds of representatives will run the government. It says what people are qualified to be representatives. The Constitution also makes sure that Americans always have the right to elect their representatives. It says how often each kind of representative must be elected.

A Federal System of Government

The delegates at the Constitutional Convention wanted the national government to be strong. But they didn't want it to be so strong that it could abuse the rights of the people. So, they set up a **federal system** of government. In a federal system, power is divided between the national—or *federal*—government and the state governments. The federal government has the power to govern the whole country. The state governments have the power to govern the states.

The Constitution lists the powers that belong only to the federal government. For example, only the federal government can declare war. The Constitution also lists the powers that the government does *not* have. For example, the government cannot tax exports or give any person a noble rank such as *king* or *queen*.

The Constitution promises that every state in the Union will have a state government based on elections. It says that all citizens have the same rights no matter what state they live in.

The Supreme Law of the Land

The delegates at the Constitutional Convention made sure that the new government had the power to run the nation and protect it from its enemies.

The Constitution says that it is the *supreme law of the land*. That means everyone who lives in the United States *must* obey the Constitution and the laws made by the federal government. If a state law goes against the Constitution, the state law must be struck down.

Looking Back
1. What is a republic?
2. How does a federal system work?
3. Why is the Constitution called the supreme law of the land?

Three Powerful Branches of Government

The delegates at the Constitutional Convention wanted to make sure that no one in the federal government could become too powerful. That is why the Constitution divides the government into three branches. Together, the three branches run the country.

Separation of Powers

The Constitution *separates* (keeps apart) the powers of the three branches. Each branch has its own certain powers. The other two branches do not have those same powers. They also cannot take away any of those powers. That separation of powers keeps one branch from becoming more powerful than another branch.

The Legislative Branch

The legislative branch makes the laws that run the country. It has the power to make all laws and set all taxes for the whole nation. It also decides how tax money should be spent.

The legislative branch is called **Congress**. The members of Congress are elected by citizens of the United States. Congress is made up of two houses—the **House of Representatives** and the **Senate**.

The Executive Branch

The executive branch has the duty to make sure the Constitution and laws of Congress are carried out. The executive branch is headed by the **President of the United States**. If something happens to the President, the **Vice-President of the United States** takes over. Both the President and Vice-President are elected by *electors*—special voters who represent the people of each state.

The Constitution gives the President powers needed to lead the nation. For example, the President has the power to command the armed forces.

The Judicial Branch

The judicial branch is made up of the **Supreme Court of the United States** and other **federal courts**. It has the power to decide court cases in which someone is accused of violating the Constitution or breaking a federal law. It also has the power to settle arguments between states.

The judges of the Supreme Court and other federal courts are chosen by the President and approved by the Senate.

Checks and Balances Limit Power

The Constitution sets up a system of **checks and balances**. Each branch has certain powers that allow it to *check*, or limit, the powers of another branch. That keeps the power of the three branches *balanced*, or equal.

For example: Suppose Congress wants the country to have a certain law. It *passes* (votes for) a *bill*. A bill is a suggestion for a law.

The bill will become a law if the President signs it. But the President does not want the law. So, the President *vetos* the bill—refuses to sign it: The President checks the power of Congress.

Congress next checks the power of the President. It *overrides* the President's veto: It votes to make the bill a law even though the President disagrees with it.

The Supreme Court then checks the power of Congress. It says the law is *unconstitutional*—it goes against the Constitution. The law is thrown out.

Looking Back
1. What are the three branches of the United States government?
2. What powers are given to
   a. the legislative branch?
   b. the executive branch?
   c. the judicial branch?
3. How is power kept balanced among the three branches?

In July 1788, New York City celebrated the ratification of the U.S. Constitution with a parade of floats. This engraving is from an early history book.

Courtesy of The New York Historical Society, New York City

The Constitution Wins Approval

Before the Constitution could become the law of the land, nine states had to *ratify*, or approve, it. Special conventions were called in each state. The delegates to those state conventions met to vote on the new Constitution.

Federalists and Anti-Federalists

People who supported the Constitution were called **Federalists**. Those people wanted a federal system of government. They believed the nation needed a strong national government. They said that the nation could not survive and solve its problems unless it had a strong government.

People who did not support the new Constitution were called **Anti-Federalists**. Anti-Federalists wanted power to remain with the state governments. They feared a strong national government. They worried that it might try to take away their rights.

The Conventions Meet

In December 1787, Delaware became the first state to ratify the Constitution. Four more states, Pennsylvania, New Jersey, Georgia, and Connecticut, soon followed.

In Massachusetts, Anti-Federalist feelings were strong. Many people were against the Constitution because it did not have a bill of rights.

The governor of Massachusetts, John Hancock, suggested a compromise: Massachusetts should approve the Constitution, then ask Congress to add a bill of rights. The delegates agreed. In February 1788, Massachusetts became the sixth state to ratify.

By June, Maryland, South Carolina, and New Hampshire had ratified the Constitution. That brought the total to nine states, enough to make the Constitution the law of the land. But two large and important states were not part of those nine states. They were Virginia and New York. In both states, Anti-Federalist feelings were strong. Federalists worked hard to win over the Anti-Federalists. They promised that a bill of rights would be added to the Constitution.

At the end of June, Virginia ratifed. Soon afterward, New York ratified.

The remaining two states of the Union eventually also ratified. North Carolina ratified in November 1789. And Rhode Island ratified in May 1790.

Looking Back

1. Why did the Federalists support the Constitution?
2. Why were the Anti-Federalists against the Constitution?
3. What did the Anti-Federalists want added to the Constitution?
4. Suppose you had been living in 1788. How would you have voted on the new Constitution? Why?

Chapter 7

Facts First

Use words below to complete each sentence.

Articles of Confederation
branches
compromise
Congress
Constitution
enslaved people
George Washington
House of Representatives
James Madison
Senate

1. In 1787, delegates met in Philadelphia to change the _____.
2. Instead, the delegates wrote the _____, a new plan of government.
3. _____ was president of the convention.
4. Many of _____'s ideas were used in the new plan.
5. The Virginia Plan called for three _____ of government.
6. Large and small states argued about representation in _____.
7. The delegates ended the argument over representation with a _____.
8. Representation in the _____ would be based on population.
9. Representation in the _____ would be equal.
10. Three-fifths of a state's _____ would be counted as part of the population.

Word Check

Write the meaning of each of these words. Then use each word in a sentence.

compromise   **federal**
delegate   **ratify**

Skill Builder

Make a chart like the one below.

The Three Branches of Government

Legislative	Executive	Judicial

1. Put each of these parts of government in the column where it belongs.
   President   Congress   Supreme Court
2. Find out what powers each branch has. Write those powers on the chart.

Chapter 7 Notes

Read over the chapter. Find answers to these questions:

1. Why did the states hold a convention in Philadelphia in 1787?
2. Why is James Madison called the Father of the Constitution?
3. What were the ideas of the Great Compromise?
4. What compromise did the delegates make
   a. in the three-fifths rule?
   b. about trade between states and other countries?
5. What three branches of government did the Constitution set up?
6. How does the system of checks and balances work?
7. How does the Constitution divide power between the federal and state governments?

Be a Historian

Find out about one of these delegates to the Constitutional Convention. Then report what you found.

John Dickinson   Edmund Randolph
Alexander Hamilton   John Rutledge
Rufus King   Roger Sherman
George Mason   James Wilson
Gouverneur Morris

Chapter 8 The New Federal Government

The Bettmann Archive, Inc.

George Washington took the oath of office in Federal Hall, New York City. He promised to "preserve, protect, and defend the Constitution." Every President since then has made the same oath.

The Constitution of the United States went into effect in 1789. Elections were held in each state to choose representatives to Congress. George Washington became President, and John Adams of Massachusetts became Vice-President.

The nation's leaders then organized the new federal government according to the plan described by the Constitution. That plan provided a solid base on which to build a successful system of government. Between 1789 and 1800, the nation grew stronger.

- How was the new federal government organized?
- What does the first census tell us about the American people in 1790?
- What rights and freedoms are protected by the Bill of Rights?
- How did political parties develop?

Key Words You will be using these words in this chapter. Look them up in the glossary at the back of Part 1.

amendment	**census**
cabinet	**political party**

Organizing the Government

On April 30, 1789, George Washington stood on the balcony of Federal Hall in New York City. He was about to become the first President of the United States.

Washington took the President's *oath* of office. (An oath is a promise.) He promised to "preserve, protect, and defend the Constitution."

The new President and Congress began the job of setting up the government.

Organizing Congress

The new Congress organized itself quickly. The House of Representatives chose a leader to run its meetings. That leader was called the **Speaker of the House**.

The Constitution makes the Vice-President the leader of the Senate. It says that the Vice-President is the **President of the Senate**. But the Senate also chose one of its members to act as president when the Vice-President was not there. That senator was called the **president pro tempore**, or temporary president.

Organizing the Executive Branch

Congress next helped to organize the executive branch. In 1789, Congress passed laws that set up three departments to help the President.

The first department was the **State Department**. Its job was to take care of *foreign affairs*—the nation's dealings with other countries. The President asked Thomas Jefferson to be *Secretary of State*, or head of the State Department.

Congress also set up the **Department of the Treasury**. Its job was to take care of the nation's financial affairs: It collected taxes. It made sure tax money was spent as Congress voted to spend it. And it could borrow money for the government and repay government debts. The President chose **Alexander Hamilton** of New York as the first *Secretary of the Treasury*.

Congress also set up the **Department of War**. (In 1947, it was renamed. We now call it the **Department of Defense**.) Its job was to run the nation's armed forces. **Henry Knox**, a general in the War for Independence, became the first *Secretary of War*.

President Washington asked the heads of the departments to meet with him often. They became the President's *cabinet*, or group of advisors. The Constitution does not say anything about a cabinet. But all Presidents since Washington have also asked their department heads to serve as a cabinet.

Organizing the Judicial Branch

Congress helped to organize the federal court system. The Constitution sets up the **Supreme Court**, which is the *highest*, or most powerful, court in the land. The Constitution then gives Congress the power to set up other federal courts. Those courts are called **lower federal courts**.

In 1789, Congress set up the lower federal courts. It created 13 *federal district courts*. It also set up three *circuit courts* (now called *Courts of Appeals*).

Federal courts decide cases dealing with federal laws, treaties, and the Constitution. All other cases are decided by state courts.

People who do not agree with a decision made by a lower court have the right to *appeal*. That means they can ask a higher court to look at the case again. Because the Supreme Court is the highest court, its decisions are final.

POPULATION OF THE UNITED STATES 1790

This graph shows the original nationalities of colonists who became Americans.

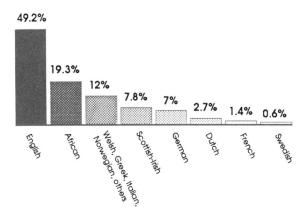

The First Census

The Constitution says that Americans must be counted every ten years. This count is called a *census*. The census is used to decide how many votes each state will have in the House of Representatives.

In 1790, the first census showed that the nation had about four million people, including 700,000 slaves. Most Americans were farmers. Only one American in 20 lived in a city. The two largest cities were Philadelphia and New York.

The census also showed that Americans came from many countries. Look at the graph at the top of the page. It shows the countries Americans came from. From which countries did most Americans come?

Looking Back

1. Who is the leader of the House of Representatives? Who is the leader of the Senate?
2. What departments did Congress set up in the executive branch? Why were they set up?
3. Who are the members of the President's cabinet?
4. Which is the highest federal court?
5. In 1790, most Americans lived on farms. Where do you think most Americans live today?

The Bill of Rights

You read in Chapter 7 that many Americans had opposed the Constitution because it did not list the rights of people. In 1789, Congress proposed ten *amendments* to the Constitution. Those amendments had to do with people's rights.

The Constitution cannot be *amended*, or added to, unless three-fourths of the states ratify the amendment. So, the ten proposed amendments were sent to the state legislatures. In 1791, the amendments were ratified by the states.

Those first ten amendments to the Constitution are known as the **Bill of Rights**.

Amendment 1: Basic Freedoms

The **First Amendment** gives Americans five basic freedoms. The first basic freedom is **freedom of religion**. The government may not force Americans to follow any religion. People are free to worship in whatever way they choose.

The second basic freedom is **freedom of speech**. People are free to say whatever they wish. People are also free to listen to any speaker they wish to hear.

The third freedom is **freedom of the press**. Publishers of newspapers, books, and magazines are free to print whatever they wish. Americans are also free to read whatever they wish.

The fourth freedom is **freedom of assembly**. (An assembly is a meeting.) The government cannot keep people from meeting, as long as their meeting is peaceful. Americans are free to meet with others for any peaceful reasons, from social activities such as dances to political activities such as protest marches.

The fifth freedom is the **right to petition the government**. Every American has the right to *petition*, or ask, the government to do something. A petition may be a letter from one person asking for help with a problem. Or it may be a written request signed by thousands of people asking for a new law.

Amendment 2: Right to Bear Arms

The **Second Amendment** says that people have the right to "bear arms" as part of "a well-regulated militia." That means states can have their own troops and those troops may have weapons.

Amendment 3: No Housing of Soldiers

Before the War for Independence, the British had forced Americans to feed and house British soldiers. The **Third Amendment** says that people cannot be forced to take soldiers into their homes during peacetime.

Amendment 4: No Unreasonable Searches

The **Fourth Amendment** protects Americans from "unreasonable searches and seizures." That means police cannot search a person or a person's property without a *search warrant*. A warrant is an order from a judge.

Americans have honored the country's first President by putting his picture on the dollar bill.

Amendments 5–8: Rights of the Accused

The next four amendments protect the rights of people accused of crimes.

The **Fifth Amendment** says that people cannot have their freedom or property taken from them without "due process of law." That means a court must follow certain legal steps to charge people or convict them of a crime. People cannot be forced to confess or to testify against themselves. And if a court finds someone innocent of a crime, that person cannot be arrested again for the same crime.

The **Sixth Amendment** gives people who are accused of crimes the right to a jury trial. That trial must take place as soon as possible. People may have a lawyer to defend them. They must be told why they were arrested. They may call witnesses to help them. And they may be in court to hear witnesses give evidence against them.

The **Seventh Amendment** states that people have the right to a jury trial in *civil cases*. Civil cases are disputes about money or property.

The **Eighth Amendment** states that a court may not set *bail* too high. Bail is money a person pays to the court in order to go free until his or her trial. The money is returned when the person appears for the trial. Courts may not force people to pay unfair fines. And courts may not punish people in cruel or unusual ways, such as by torturing them.

Amendment 9: Other Rights

Some Americans feared that the rights listed in the Bill of Rights would be the only rights they had. So, the **Ninth Amendment** was added. It says that Americans have other rights besides those listed in the Constitution. The government must respect those rights as well.

Amendment 10: Limits on Power

The **Tenth Amendment** says that powers not given to the federal government by the Constitution belong to the states or to the people. This last amendment was added to keep the national government from becoming too powerful.

The Land of the Free

When the Bill of Rights was added to the Constitution in 1791, most people in the world did not have the rights it listed.

Even today, people in many countries do not have the rights and freedoms *guaranteed* (promised) to Americans in the Bill of Rights. For example, people in some countries do not have the right to worship freely. They cannot speak out against their government without fear of arrest. And if they are arrested, they may be kept in jail for years without a trial.

The Bill of Rights protects Americans from such abuses. Because of the freedoms guaranteed in the Bill of Rights, America is called the "land of the free."

Looking Back

1. List the five freedoms protected in the First Amendment.
2. How does the Fourth Amendment protect Americans?
3. List some rights of people accused of a crime.
4. Suppose you think that someone has taken away the rights promised you in the Bill of Rights. What can you do?

The Rise of Political Parties

George Washington served for eight years as President. During that time, two *political parties* developed in the nation. They were the **Federalist Party** and the **Democratic-Republican Party**.

A political party is a group of people sharing the same ideas about government. Those people try to get certain laws passed. They also try to get certain people elected to government office.

The Federalist Party

The Federalist Party was led by Alexander Hamilton, the Secretary of the Treasury. Federalists favored a strong federal government. They believed that only a strong government could enforce its laws and keep order in the country. Federalists also believed government should be run by the "best people." By that, they meant people with property and education. As one Federalist leader, John Jay, said, "Those who own the country ought to govern it."

Members of the Federalist Party were often businessmen. Many lived in the New England states and in the busy port cities along the Atlantic coast. They wanted the government to pass laws that would help businesses grow.

The Democratic-Republican Party

The Democratic-Republican Party was led by Thomas Jefferson, the Secretary of State. Members of that party feared a strong federal government. They believed that most of the power should be held by the states. They wanted to limit the power of the federal government. Democratic-Republicans believed that *all* people, not just the rich, should have a say in running their government. People of many different backgrounds, including businessmen and farmers, supported the party. Many of them lived in the South and the West.

The Battle over the National Bank

In 1790, Federalists and Democratic-Republicans strongly disagreed about whether Congress should set up a **national bank**.

The national bank was Alexander Hamilton's idea. Hamilton wanted a strong bank that could help the nation grow. The government would keep tax money it collected in that bank. Hamilton said the national bank could also help business people and merchants by lending them money. Federalists agreed with Hamilton's idea.

Jefferson and other Democratic-Republicans protested. Jefferson argued that the Constitution said nothing about giving Congress the power to set up a bank. If the Constitution did not say the government could do something, then it should not be done, he said.

But Hamilton and the Federalists said that the Constitution *did* give Congress the power to set up a bank. Hamilton made this argument: The Constitution cannot list all the things a government might need to do. So, the Constitution says that Congress can "make all the laws which shall be necessary" to carry out the government's powers. The government has the power to collect taxes. A national bank is "necessary" to help the Treasury Department carry out that power.

Hamilton's arguments won out. In 1791, Congress passed a law setting up the Bank of the United States.

The Whiskey Rebellion

In 1791, Secretary of the Treasury Hamilton convinced Congress to pass a series of new taxes to raise money. One of those taxes was a tax on whiskey.

The whiskey tax especially angered farmers in western Pennsylvania. Those farmers grew grain to make money.

This engraving shows angry farmers during the Whiskey Rebellion. They have put tar and feathers on a tax collector.

But sacks of grain were heavy and hard to ship. So, the farmers made much of their grain into whiskey. Whiskey was easier to ship and sold at a good price.

If the farmers paid the whiskey tax, they would make less money. Many of them rebelled: They refused to pay the tax and they attacked tax collectors.

President Washington moved quickly to put down the **Whiskey Rebellion**. He wanted to show Americans that the federal government was strong enough to keep law and order in the nation. Washington organized an army of 15,000 troops. In 1794, the army marched into western Pennsylvania. The rebel leaders fled and the rebellion ended.

Federalists were pleased with this show of federal power. But western farmers were angry. In the next presidential election, they supported the Democratic-Republicans.

The Parties Compete for Power

In 1796, President Washington decided not to run for a third term. (A President's term is four years. Washington had served for two terms, or eight years.) As he left office, Washington warned Americans that political parties were dividing the nation. He hoped the parties would disappear.

Instead, political parties became more important. In the election of 1796, Federalists backed **John Adams** for President. The Democratic-Republicans supported Thomas Jefferson. Members of each party worked hard to win the election. Each party held *rallies*, or meetings, to stir up support for their candidate.

The Federalists won the election and John Adams became President.

In the next presidential election, four years later, Federalists again supported John Adams. Democratic-Republicans again supported Thomas Jefferson. This time the Democratic-Republicans were stronger. Jefferson was elected President in 1800.

President Jefferson hoped to bring Federalists and Democratic-Republicans together. In his first speech he said, ''We are all Republicans—we are all Federalists.''

But Americans continued to have different beliefs about government. And they continued to support different political parties. As the nation grew, political parties became more powerful. They became an important part of the way Americans choose their leaders.

Looking Back

1. What kind of national government did the Federalists want?
2. What kind of national government did the Democratic-Republicans want?
3. Who were the leaders of the Federalist and Democratic-Republican parties? What kind of people did each want to run the government?
4. Why were Democratic-Republicans against the national bank?
5. Why did Washington act quickly to put down the Whiskey Rebellion?
6. What political parties are important in the United States today?

Chapter 8

Review

Facts First

Complete each sentence by choosing the correct ending.

1. To organize the executive branch, Congress set up
   a. the departments of State, Treasury, and War.
   b. committees of the Senate.
   c. the lower federal courts.

2. Lower federal courts were set up by
   a. the President.
   b. Congress.
   c. the states.

3. The 1790 census showed that
   a. most Americans lived on farms.
   b. most Americans lived in cities.
   c. most Americans were slaves.

4. The Bill of Rights is
   a. part of the Declaration of Independence.
   b. the first ten amendments to the U.S. Constitution.
   c. a law that never passed.

5. The First Amendment gives people
   a. five basic freedoms.
   b. freedom from taxes.
   c. a list of duties.

6. During the Whiskey Rebellion, the new government showed it
   a. was weak.
   b. was strong enough to govern.
   c. would abuse people's rights.

7. Political parties
   a. help choose government leaders.
   b. never caught on in America.
   c. were against the law.

Word Check

Write the meanings of these words. Then use them in sentences.

amendment	**census**
cabinet	**political party**

Skill Builder

Make a chart that compares the nation's first political parties.

1. Write this title at the top of the chart: **America's First Political Parties**

2. Make two columns. Write *Federalist Party* at the top of one column. Write *Democratic-Republican Party* at the top of the other column.

3. Fill in your chart by answering these questions. Answer each question for *both* parties.
   - Who was their leader?
   - What kind of people did they want as government leaders?
   - What kind of national government did they want?
   - How did they feel about a national bank?
   - Who was their choice for President in 1796?

Chapter 8 Notes

Read over the chapter. Find answers to these questions:

1. Who is the leader of the House of Representatives? Who is President of the Senate? Who leads the Senate if the President of the Senate is absent?

2. What did the first census show about the American people in 1790?

3. What rights and freedoms are protected by the Bill of Rights?

4. What did Federalists want from the national government?

5. What kind of government did Democratic-Republicans want?

Be a Historian

Find out which political party your classmates, friends, and neighbors support. Ask this question: ''Which political party do you usually support in an election?''

Unit 3

Review

What Do You Know?

Complete each sentence by choosing the correct ending.

1. After independence was won, new state constitutions
   a. set up representative governments.
   b. freed all slaves in America.
   c. gave women all the same rights as men.

2. Under the Articles of Confederation,
   a. the national government was weak.
   b. the states had little power.
   c. states worked together well.

3. Delegates at the Constitutional Convention
   a. wrote a new plan of government.
   b. agreed about everything.
   c. refused to compromise.

4. Under the Constitution, each state had
   a. one representative in the Supreme Court.
   b. two representatives in the Senate.
   c. one representative in Parliament.

5. The Constitution
   a. gave the states all the power.
   b. divided power between the national government and the states.
   c. set up a weak national government.

6. The Bill of Rights
   a. ended slavery in America.
   b. listed people's rights and freedoms.
   c. gave women the right to vote.

7. As the nation grew, political parties became
   a. a way for Congress to raise taxes.
   b. an important part of the way Americans choose their leaders.
   c. important to keeping law and order.

What Do You Think?

Some people today think that the national government has grown too powerful. They say the government has too much control over people's lives at home, at work, and elsewhere. What do you think?

Skill Builder

Find out in what years these documents were written. Then write them in order.
- The Constitution
- The Land Ordinance of 1785
- The Bill of Rights
- The Articles of Confederation
- The Declaration of Independence
- The Northwest Ordinance

Unit 3 Notes

Look over the unit to find answers to these questions:

1. Why was the earliest national government a weak one?

2. What problems did the country have because of its weak government?

3. What compromises were made in writing the Constitution?

4. How was the federal government organized under the Constitution?

5. Why was the Bill of Rights added to the Constitution?

6. What kind of national government did the first American political parties want?

Word Builder

Write a story about the Constitution. Use all the key words listed below.

Key Words

amendment	delegate
cabinet	election
census	national
compromise	ratify

unit 4 The New Nation Begins to Grow

Montana—August 17, 1805

A Shoshone Indian woman walks rapidly next to a river high in the Rocky Mountains. Following behind are two men: her husband, a fur trader who is half French and half Indian, and William Clark, an officer in the United States Army. In the river next to them, other army men struggle to paddle six canoes against the fast-moving water.

The woman's name is Sacajawea, and she is sixteen years old. She and the men are all members of an *expedition*—a group of people sent to explore unknown lands. Their leaders are Captain William Clark and Captain Meriwether Lewis.

Captain Lewis and three men left the group a week ago to look for the Shoshone Indians who live on these lands. The expedition needs horses to get over the mountains. Lewis hopes to buy the horses from the Shoshone.

Sacajawea is excited. The Shoshone who live here are her people. As a child, she was captured in an Indian war. She has not seen these lands or her people for five years.

Sacajawea sees Shoshone Indians on horseback. Captain Lewis is with them. The Shoshone take the members of the expedition to the Indian camp. A crowd of Shoshone surround them, and the men become fearful. They hold their weapons tightly, ready to defend themselves. Suddenly, a woman pushes her way through the crowd toward Sacajawea, calling to her. Sacajawea recognizes the woman and cries out. She rushes forward, and the women hug each other joyfully. The men smile and relax; they know the Shoshone will not harm them.

In Our Time

The story you just read really did happen. Sacajawea was a real person. She helped Lewis and Clark buy the horses they needed. We know about Sacajawea and her story because both Lewis and Clark kept *journals*. A journal is a kind of diary that a person writes in every day.

When people write journals, they tell what happened during the day. They tell the latest news. Years later, those journals help us learn the history of their time.

Today, people still keep journals. Sometimes they write their journals in books, the way Lewis and Clark did. Sometimes they put their journals on cassette tapes or videotapes.

What are some journals you've read, heard, or seen?

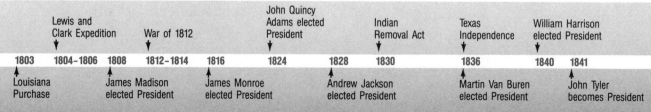

	Lewis and Clark Expedition		War of 1812		John Quincy Adams elected President		Indian Removal Act		Texas Independence		William Harrison elected President	
1803	1804–1806	1808	1812–1814	1816	1824	1828	1830		1836		1840	1841
Louisiana Purchase		James Madison elected President		James Monroe elected President		Andrew Jackson elected President			Martin Van Buren elected President			John Tyler becomes President

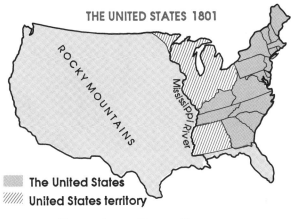

THE UNITED STATES 1801

ROCKY MOUNTAINS

Mississippi River

▓ **The United States**
▨ **United States territory**

The American Frontier

During the 1770s and 1780s, Americans were fighting the War for Independence and building a new nation. Only a few thousand *pioneers* crossed the Appalachian Mountains. The land from the Appalachians to the Mississippi River was America's *frontier*.

The first pioneers to move onto the frontier were usually hunters and trappers such as **Daniel Boone**. They followed Indian paths over the Appalachians. They hacked out trails through wilderness. Slowly, those trails and paths were widened into roads.

The roads made it possible for people to travel over the mountains by wagon. So, during the 1790s, thousands of pioneer families packed their goods into covered wagons and headed west.

The Journey over the Mountains

The journey across the Appalachian Mountains was difficult and dangerous. Pioneer families traveled along rough dirt roads that were deeply cut by ruts and holes. Their wagons often got stuck in muddy places and had to be pushed out. They came to rivers and streams that they had to cross. Sometimes, their horses and wagons were swept away by the water.

Many settlers who made the journey west did not want to return to the East. Travelers joked that the reason was "not that the western country is so good, but that the journey back is so bad."

Looking Back

1. Where did pioneers begin to settle after the War for Independence?
2. Who were the first pioneers?
3. *Map work*: Look at a large map of the United States today. Find the areas that the five nations claimed in 1801.

Chapter ⑨ **The Frontier**

In 1801, Thomas Jefferson was President. Five nations claimed parts of North America. They were the United States, France, Spain, Britain, and Russia. Vast areas of land were still unsettled.

The United States claimed land south of Canada, from the Atlantic Ocean to the Mississippi River (except for Florida).

France claimed most of the territory between the Mississippi River and the Rocky Mountains. That land was called the Louisiana Territory.

Spain claimed Florida as well as the New Mexico and California regions. Britain claimed the Oregon region. (Britain also claimed most of Canada from the Atlantic to the Pacific.) And Russia claimed Alaska far to the north.

- What was life like along the frontier?
- How did the United States come to own the Louisiana Territory?
- Why was the expedition of Lewis and Clark important?
- What kinds of settlements did Spain build in its territories?

Key Words   You will be using these words in this chapter. Look them up in the glossary at the back of Part 1.

disease	frontier
expedition	**pioneer**

James Polk elected President		Mexican War		California gold rush
↓		↓		↓
1844	1846	1846–1848	1848	1849
	↑		↑	
	Oregon Treaty		Zachary Taylor elected President	

In the 1790s, the American frontier was the land west of the Appalachian Mountains. This engraving shows a log cabin on the frontier.

Life on the Frontier

After the hard journey west, the pioneers faced the difficult job of building new homes and planting crops. Most frontier families settled in valleys west of the Appalachians. Thick forests grew in the valleys. Before the families could plant their first crops, they had to clear the land of trees. Then they planted crops such as corn, beans, and squash.

The trees they cut were used to build the family's first home, a log cabin. Most log cabins were very small, with only one room. The cabin had a dirt floor and tiny windows. At one end of the cabin was a fireplace made of mud or clay. The cooking was done there.

The cabin was furnished with a few wooden stools and a table. Some cabins had beds, but many families slept on the floor on animal skins.

Disease on the Frontier

Disease was a constant problem on the frontier. It was difficult to keep germs from spreading. And some frontier practices even helped them spread. For example, everybody—the sick and the healthy—drank from the same water cup. In that way, disease could spread quickly among settlers.

There were not many doctors along the frontier to treat the sick. So, settlers took care of one another. For example, settlers knew that cobwebs placed over a wound helped stop the bleeding. And settlers found that Indian medicines made from plants helped cure some illnesses.

Frontier Gatherings

Frontier life was hard and lonely. Most families lived miles away from their nearest neighbors. But families got together to help each other and have fun.

Work brought people together. When a family needed help clearing a field or putting up a barn, they got word to their neighbors. Neighbors from miles around came to help. Often they divided into teams and made a contest out of the job. When the work was done, everyone sat down to a hearty meal. Then there was singing and dancing.

The biggest frontier gatherings were for weddings. A wedding ceremony was often followed by two days of celebrating. Such occasions made the hard life of the frontier easier.

Looking Back
1. What was a frontier home like?
2. Why did disease spread quickly among settlers?
3. How did frontier families have fun?
4. Would you have enjoyed life as a pioneer? Why or why not?

The Louisiana Territory

West of the Mississippi River lay a vast, unexplored area. That area was called the **Louisiana Territory**. It stretched from the Mississippi River to the Rocky Mountains, and from Spanish Texas to British Canada.

France first claimed the territory in 1682. In 1763, at the end of the French and Indian War, France gave the land to Spain. But in 1800, Spain returned the territory to France.

America Worries about France

The news that France again controlled the Louisiana Territory worried many Americans. France was ruled by the emperor **Napoleon Bonaparte**. Napoleon had taken over many countries in Europe and was building an empire there. Americans feared that Napoleon might also want to build a French empire in America.

Western farmers were especially worried about the French. You read in Chapter 6 that the Spanish had closed the Mississippi River to Americans in 1784. Western farmers had then been unable to use the river and the port of New Orleans to ship their crops to buyers. That problem had been ended by a treaty with the Spanish. But now western farmers feared new trouble—from the French. If France closed New Orleans to Americans, once again those farmers would have no way to get their crops to market.

In 1803, President Thomas Jefferson sent **James Monroe** to France. Monroe had been the United States representative to France under George Washington. Monroe's duty now was to speak to Napoleon about selling New Orleans to the United States.

Bad News for France from Haiti

Monroe arrived in France soon after Napoleon received bad news from the Caribbean.

In 1801, Napoleon had sent about 25,000 French troops to Haiti, a French island in the Caribbean Sea. The troops had been sent to crush a slave rebellion.

But the French troops had failed. Thousands of them had died of yellow fever. The rebels, led by a former slave named **Toussaint L'Ouverture**, had destroyed the weakened French army.

A Stunning Offer

Napoleon had planned to send thousands of farmers to the Louisiana Territory. They would raise food for the slaves of Haiti. But now that he had lost Haiti, he had no use for Louisiana.

Napoleon made Monroe a stunning offer: For $15 million, he would sell not only New Orleans, but all of the Louisiana Territory. Without waiting for approval from the President, Monroe agreed to the terms of Napoleon's offer.

President Jefferson was pleased with the news that Monroe brought back to the United States. Suddenly, Jefferson had a chance to double the size of the United States. And the 15 million dollar price was a bargain: The Louisiana Territory was so huge that the cost came to only about two cents an acre.

Looking Back
1. Where was the Louisiana Territory?
2. Why did the United States want the Louisiana Territory?
3. Why was Napoleon willing to sell Louisiana?

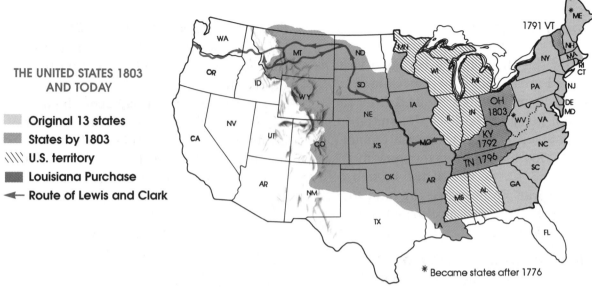

THE UNITED STATES 1803
AND TODAY

Original 13 states
States by 1803
\\\\ U.S. territory
Louisiana Purchase
← Route of Lewis and Clark

* Became states after 1776

The Louisiana Purchase

President Jefferson wanted the United States to buy the Louisiana Territory. But he had a problem: He was a Democratic-Republican who believed in limited government powers. He believed that the federal government should not do anything that was not listed in the Constitution. And the Constitution said nothing about buying such a large piece of land.

Jefferson's first idea was to amend the Constitution. The amendment would give Congress the power to buy land from other countries. But an amendment could take months or years, and Napoleon might change his mind any minute about selling the territory. Jefferson decided the land was more important than his beliefs. He asked Congress to approve the **Louisiana Purchase**.

Many Federalists opposed the purchase. They feared that the nation was becoming too large. They did not think settlers west of the Mississippi could be governed from Washington, D.C. They also complained about the price. A Federalist newspaper reported that it would take 25 ships to carry $15 million in silver to France.

Jefferson did his best to convince Congress that the Louisiana Territory was a bargain. He told them about a report he had heard: Somewhere out there, it said, was a pure white mountain of salt. That mountain alone was worth $15 million. But the Federalists had their doubts.

Congress Votes Yes

The argument went on for months. In late 1803, Congress voted in favor of the Louisiana Purchase.

After the United States bought Louisiana, Americans slowly began to explore and settle their new territory. They never found the mountain of salt. But the territory turned out to have other riches. It had some of the best soil in North America. And it was rich in oil, natural gas, and minerals such as gold, silver, copper, and iron.

Looking Back

1. Why did President Jefferson believe he should *not* buy the Louisiana Territory?
2. Why did Jefferson go against his own beliefs to buy the Louisiana Territory?
3. Why were some Federalists against the Louisiana Purchase?

The Lewis and Clark Expedition

In the spring of 1804, President Jefferson sent an *expedition* to explore the Louisiana Territory and to find a land and water route to the Pacific Ocean. Forty-three people began the expedition. It was led by two army officers, **Meriwether Lewis** and **William Clark**.

Lewis and Clark planned to go by boat up the Missouri River to the Rocky Mountains, then cross the mountains and travel to the Pacific.

Along the way, they would take notes about the land, climate, plants, and animals of the territory. They would also learn about the Indians they met.

Traveling up the Missouri

The expedition left St. Louis, Missouri, on May 14, 1804. The journey up the Missouri River was hard, hot work. The boats had to be rowed or pulled against the river's strong current.

After five months, the expedition reached what is now North Dakota. There they spent the winter of 1804–1805 with the Mandan Indians.

During that winter, a fur trader named Toussaint Charbonneau and his 16-year-old wife **Sacajawea** joined the expedition as interpreters. Sacajawea was a Shoshone Indian who had been captured by the Mandans five years earlier.

This special U.S. postage stamp was issued in 1954.

To the Pacific

When spring came, Lewis and Clark continued their journey. By August, they had reached the Rocky Mountains. They could no longer use their boats. To get across the mountains, they would need horses and Indian guides.

Lewis found some Shoshone, hoping to buy horses from them, but they did not trust him. Then Sacajawea discovered that the chief of the Shoshone was her brother. As an interpreter, she was able to help Lewis and Clark ask her brother to provide horses and guides for the expedition.

Lewis and Clark crossed the Rockies and continued west. They reached the Snake River in what is now Idaho. They built boats and traveled down the Snake River to the Columbia River in what is now Washington. By December, they had reached the Pacific.

The Journey Home

In the spring of 1806, Lewis and Clark began the journey home. The expedition finally reached St. Louis in September of that year. Lewis and Clark had been gone over two years and had traveled nearly 8000 miles. They brought back valuable information about the West.

The Lewis and Clark expedition was also very important for the growth of the nation. The journey down the Columbia River gave the United States a claim to new territory—the **Oregon Country**. And the expedition opened up a new frontier for American settlers.

Looking Back

1. What was the purpose of the Lewis and Clark expedition?
2. How did Sacajawea help the expedition?
3. *Map work*: What states today are in the old Louisiana Territory? (See page 64 map.)

The Spanish Frontier

West of the Louisiana Territory lay a huge area claimed by Spain. Spain's territory there stretched from Texas to the Pacific Ocean and from Mexico north through California.

The Spanish Southwest

The first Spanish settlements in that territory were in the Southwest, in present-day New Mexico. There the Spanish settled on land that belonged to the Pueblo Indians. In 1680, the Pueblo rebelled and drove the Spanish out. But the Spanish returned and conquered the Pueblo. By 1800, the largest Spanish settlements were in New Mexico.

Elsewhere in the Southwest, Spanish settlements remained small and scattered. In what is now Texas and Arizona, Indian peoples such as the Apache and the Comanche fought against Spanish settlement. Few settlers wished to live on the dangerous Spanish frontier.

Spanish California

For many years, the Spanish paid little attention to their territory in California. Then, in 1769, an expedition of soldiers and priests arrived in San Diego, California.

The expedition's leader was a soldier named **Gaspar de Portola**. Portola and his soldiers built their first forts in San Diego and Monterey. While exploring near Monterey, Portola discovered San Francisco Bay.

The priests, led by Father **Junipero Serra**, set up missions along the California coast. The priests wanted to teach the Catholic faith to the Indians there.

This drawing of Mission San Francisco de Asis was made by a British visitor in 1826.

At the missions, the priests taught the Indians about that religion. They also gave the Indians food, clothing, and shelter. In return, the Indians had to do the work of the mission. They raised cattle and horses and planted crops, such as wheat and grapes.

Soon, pioneers from Mexico began to settle the open grasslands near California's coast. Most of the settlers lived on *ranchos*, or large ranches. There they raised horses and cattle.

The *rancheros*, or ranch owners, often forced Indians to work on the ranches. Hard work killed many Indians. Others caught diseases such as smallpox, measles, and diphtheria that were brought by the Spanish. By 1848, a large number of the California Indians had died.

Looking Back

1. Where was the western territory claimed by Spain?
2. Why did few Spanish settle in the Southwest?
3. What do you think life was like on the Spanish missions?

Chapter 9

Review

Facts First

Use words below to complete each sentence.

California Indians missions
disease Oregon Country
Federalists Pacific Ocean
Louisiana Purchase Thomas Jefferson

1. Frontier families had constant problems with _____.
2. _____ wanted to make the Louisiana Purchase even though he felt the government was not given that power by the Constitution.
3. _____ feared the Louisiana Territory would make America too large.
4. Congress approved the _____ in late 1803.
5. Lewis and Clark explored for two years in the area between St. Louis and the _____.
6. The U.S. claimed the territory called the _____ after Lewis and Clark's expedition.
7. The Spanish built forts and _____ in California.
8. Forced work and disease killed many _____.

Word Check

Write the meaning of each of these words. Then use each word in a sentence.

  disease frontier
  expedition pioneer

Skill Builder

Lewis and Clark traveled across the West to the Pacific Ocean. Trace their route on a map of the United States.
- Begin at St. Louis where the Missouri River joins the Mississippi River.
- Follow the Missouri River north and west until it reaches the Rockies.
- Cross the Rocky Mountains. Travel west to the Snake River.
- Follow the Snake River west to the Columbia River.
- Follow the Columbia River west to the Pacific coast.

Chapter 9 Notes

Read over the chapter. Find answers to these questions:
1. How did early pioneers travel west over the Appalachian Mountains?
2. What was frontier life like?
3. What were the arguments for *and* against making the Louisiana Purchase?
4. What did the U.S. gain from the expedition of Lewis and Clark?
5. Describe life in Spanish settlements in their southwest and California territories.

Be a Historian

American families still move often in their search for a better life. Find out about the moves your family, or some members of it, made. Where did they move? Why?

Bonus

Find out about one of these important people from America's past. Then report what you learned.

Daniel Boone Sacajawea
William Clark Father Junipero Serra
Meriwether Lewis

Chapter 10   A Changing Nation

Library of Congress

A wood turner, at the beginning of the 1800s, works at his lathe.

Thomas Jefferson left the White House in 1809. By then, the United States was growing rapidly. Americans were beginning to change their way of life. Many were leaving their farms and moving to towns.

New inventions began to change how Americans produced goods. The inventions also led to the spread of cotton plantations across the South.

The nation continued to have problems with Britain. Although the Americans now had huge territories in North America, the British were still in Canada and in the far West.

Then Britain went to war with France. That war seriously threatened the rights of Americans.

- What was the Industrial Revolution and how did it begin in America?
- Why did the United States go to war again with Britain?
- Why did sections of the country begin to quarrel after the war?

Key Words   You will be using these words in this chapter. Look them up in the glossary at the back of Part 1.

factory	**produce**
invent	**section**

The Industrial Revolution Comes to the United States

In Unit 2, you read about the American Revolution. That was a *political revolution* that completely changed the American government. Around 1800, another kind of revolution began. Americans began to completely change the way they made things, worked, and lived. That revolution is called the **Industrial Revolution.**

The Rise of Factories

Before the Industrial Revolution, people made most of the things they needed at home or in small shops. Most Americans lived on farms. Farm families grew their own food. They wove their own cloth and sewed their own clothes. They made their own soap and medicines. They built their own furniture and farm tools.

Then people began to *invent* machines that could help them do hard work and make things faster. Soon, people began building *factories*. The factories used machines to *produce* things that people had been making at home. The factories also needed workers to run the machines, and many Americans began leaving their farms. They moved to towns to work in the factories there.

The Textile Mills

An important business in New England was *textiles*—making thread and cloth. Thread and cloth were spun and woven by hand in small shops. Then, in 1789, an English textile worker named **Samuel Slater** came to America. He carried plans in his head for making machines that could spin cotton into thread. In 1790, Slater helped set up a *spinning mill* in Rhode Island. The spinning mill was a factory that used machines to spin thread. Soon, other spinning mills sprang up throughout New England.

Around 1814, a businessman named **Francis Cabot Lowell** built a mill in Massachusetts to produce thread. But he also put *power looms* in his mill. The power looms were machines that could weave thread into cloth. Lowell's mill became the first complete textile factory: It turned raw cotton into thread, then thread into cloth.

The Cotton Gin

The cotton for New England's textile factories came from the South, where it was grown on plantations. Slaves picked the cotton by hand from cotton plants. Then they pulled out seeds from the cotton, also by hand. It was slow work. A slave could clean only about one pound of cotton a day.

Eli Whitney, an inventor from New England, invented a machine in 1793. He called it a *cotton engine*. The name was soon shortened to **cotton gin**. The cotton gin was operated by hand. It quickly separated seeds from cotton fibers. A single worker using the cotton gin could clean 50 pounds of cotton in a day.

King Cotton

The invention of the cotton gin brought changes to the South. Cotton soon became its most important crop. Planters discovered they could make more money selling cotton than tobacco. They now wanted more land to grow cotton. Many moved west to start huge cotton plantations in present-day Alabama, Mississippi, and Louisiana. They took thousands of slaves with them to grow and pick the cotton on those plantations.

The planters sold their cotton to textile mills in Britain as well as New England. Soon, cotton became the most valuable export from the United States. Southerners called cotton the "king" of crops.

Mass Production

In 1798, Eli Whitney came up with another new idea. He started a gun factory in New England and began to make guns by a new method. Until then, guns had been made by skilled gunsmiths, one at a time. No two guns were exactly alike because each part of the gun was carefully shaped by hand. So, making guns took a long time, and guns were expensive to buy.

Whitney invented machines that workers used to make all the gun parts. With those machines, workers could make thousands of parts that were *identical* (exactly alike). For example, all the triggers were identical, and all the barrels were identical. To make a gun, Whitney simply put all the different gun parts together. In that way, he could quickly make a gun.

Whitney's system of identical parts made the **mass production** of guns possible—he could quickly produce large numbers of them. Mass-produced guns were cheaper than handmade guns. They were also easier to repair: New parts could be ordered from the factory.

Other people began to use Whitney's system. For example, a clockmaker named Eli Terry used it to make clocks. His factory-made clocks cost only a few dollars. Handmade clocks cost as much as $20. Soon, Americans were buying many things that were factory-made, such as furniture, tools, and cloth.

Looking Back

1. How did factories change the way things were made?
2. Why did many people move to towns?
3. How did the invention of the cotton gin change the South?
4. What new idea did Eli Whitney use in his gun factory?
5. Why did Americans begin to buy factory-made goods?

The War of 1812 (1812-1814)

In 1809, James Madison became the nation's fourth President. He soon faced a number of serious and growing problems with Britain on the seas and on the western frontier. Britain still controlled Canada.

America Wants to Be Neutral

Britain and France had been at war since 1793. Both nations wanted to buy food and supplies from the United States. And each nation wanted to stop American ships from taking supplies to the other. The British navy captured American merchant ships going to France. At the same time, the French navy captured American ships heading for British ports.

America was *neutral* in the war. That meant that it did not favor either side. The American government protested to Britain and France, saying that neutral ships should be free to trade with any nation.

The British Impress Americans

Americans also protested the British practice of *impressment*. Impressment was the practice of forcing people to serve in the navy.

The British often stopped American merchant ships to look for British sailors working for the Americans. The British claimed that, in time of war, it was the duty of all British sailors to serve their country. So, they took those they found on American ships to serve in the British navy. Sometimes, they took American sailors as well.

Trouble in the West

Americans were also having problems on the western frontier. Fighting between Indians and American settlers increased. Then, in 1811, a war broke out on the frontier. A Shawnee chief named **Tecumseh** united the Indians of the Northwest Territory against the settlers.

The governor of the Indiana Territory, **William Henry Harrison**, led about 1000 troops against Tecumseh's forces. Harrison's forces destroyed the Indians' camp on Tippecanoe Creek in western Indiana.

British guns were found on the battlefield at Tippecanoe. The settlers believed the British had given those guns to the Indians. Americans were convinced there would be no peace until the British were out of Canada.

The War Hawks

When Congress met in 1811, **Henry Clay** was Speaker of the House. There were several new young members from the South and the West. Those young Congressmen, led by Henry Clay, wanted to go to war against Britain. For that reason, they were called **War Hawks**.

The War Hawks saw three reasons for going to war: The first was to protect free trade and the rights of American sailors. The second was to end Indian attacks on western settlers. The third was to increase American territory by capturing Canada.

On June 16, 1812, the British government ordered its navy to stop attacking American ships. But that news did not reach America in time. On June 18, Congress declared war on Britain.

Looking Back
1. Why did British warships stop American merchant ships? What did they do with the sailors on those ships?
2. What problem did the United States have with Britain in the West?
3. Who were the War Hawks?

The War in Canada

The War Hawks thought the war would be easy to win. But they were wrong. The American army was small and unprepared. The American navy had few battleships, while Britain had over 100.

In 1812 and 1813, the Americans tried to invade Canada several times. But they were not successful.

Britain Invades the United States

In 1814, Britain won its war with France. British troops were then sent to America. Britain planned to attack the United States in three places: It would invade New York from Canada. It would attack Washington, D.C. And it would capture New Orleans in the South.

The U.S. Capital Is Burned

The Americans stopped the British invasion from Canada. But they could not stop the invasion of Washington. In August 1814, British troops captured the capital and set fire to the White House.

British forces then moved north from Washington and attacked Ft. McHenry near Baltimore, Maryland. For a day and night, they bombed the fort. But the Americans held Ft. McHenry and stopped the British advance.

On a ship in Baltimore harbor, **Francis Scott Key** watched through the night as the British attacked Ft. McHenry. At dawn, he was thrilled to see an American flag still waving over the fort. He put down his feelings in ''The Star Spangled Banner.''

Disaster for the British at New Orleans

On January 8, 1815, the British attacked New Orleans. The battle was a disaster for the British. American General **Andrew Jackson** had put together an army of free blacks and Indian fighters to defend the city. The British lost 2000 soldiers, while the Americans lost only 21.

Library of Congress

The British bombed Fort McHenry near Baltimore in the War of 1812. The Americans won after an all-night battle. This drawing shows the fort under fire.

The Treaty of Ghent

The Battle of New Orleans was actually fought after the war was over. Two weeks earlier, Britain and the United States had signed a peace treaty in Ghent, Belgium. News of the **Treaty of Ghent** did not reach America until February.

The Treaty of Ghent presented the terms of peace. In the treaty, Britain and the United States kept all their territories. The War of 1812 was the last time the United States and Britain fought each other. In the future, they would solve their problems through peaceful talks, instead of war.

Looking Back

1. How did Francis Scott Key share his feelings about the American victory at Ft. McHenry?
2. What did the Treaty of Ghent say about U.S. and British territories?
3. How are arguments between the U.S. and Britain handled differently today than in the 1700s and 1812?

The Growth of Sectionalism

After the War of 1812, a new spirit of *nationalism* swept the country. Nationalism is a feeling of deep pride in one's country.

The spirit of nationalism destroyed the Federalist Party. Too many Federalists had opposed the war. Many Americans believed Federalists were *unpatriotic*, or unwilling to support their country.

The Era of Good Feelings

In 1816, Americans backed the Democratic-Republican Party and its presidential candidate, James Monroe. Monroe easily became the nation's fifth President.

After taking office, President Monroe toured the country. A Boston newspaper called his trip the start of an "era of good feelings." Never had the nation seemed more united.

North and South Disagree

The "era of good feelings" did not last. By 1820, unity was disappearing from the nation. Differences and arguments between *sections* of the country—the North and South—divided the nation. That caused **sectionalism**: People were loyal to sections and not to the whole country.

The North and the South were divided over slavery. Most northerners were against slavery. They felt that slavery had no place in a nation that believed in liberty for all.

Most southerners defended slavery. They saw nothing wrong with it. Southerners believed that, without slave labor, they could not plant and raise their crops on the huge areas of the plantations.

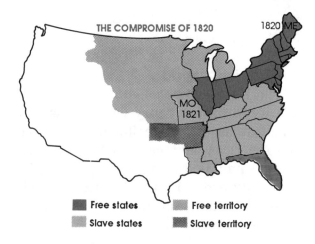

THE COMPROMISE OF 1820

1820 ME
MO 1821

■ Free states ▨ Free territory
▨ Slave states ▧ Slave territory

The Missouri Compromise

The nation had grown to 22 states: 11 slave states (states that allowed slavery) and 11 free states (states without slavery). That meant that slave and free states had the same number of votes in the Senate.

In 1818, the Missouri Territory asked to become a state. Missouri permitted slavery. If it became a state, the slave states would have more votes in the Senate.

Throughout 1819, Congress argued about admitting Missouri to the Union. Then, in 1820, the territory of Maine asked to be admitted as a free state. An agreement was reached. That agreement was called the **Missouri Compromise**.

Under the Missouri Compromise, Missouri was admitted as a slave state. Maine was admitted as a free state. That kept the balance between slave and free states in the Senate.

To settle future arguments about slavery in the territories, Congress divided the Louisiana Territory. Slavery was forbidden in the North (except in Missouri). Slavery was allowed in the South.

Looking Back

1. What did northerners and southerners believe about slavery?
2. What did the Missouri Compromise do?
3. *Map work*: Find out the names of the free states and the slave states in 1820.

Rule by the Common Man

In the original 13 states of the nation, only property owners could vote. And men who were wealthy and educated were elected to office.

But Vermont helped change that. Vermont, which became the fourteenth state in 1791, gave the vote to any adult man. Other states joining the Union followed Vermont's example. More ''common people''—neither wealthy nor highly educated—began to vote.

The Election of 1824

In the presidential election of 1824, four people ran for President: William Crawford, John Quincy Adams, Henry Clay, and Andrew Jackson.

Jackson got the most votes but he did not win a *majority* (more than half). The Constitution gives the House of Representatives the power to choose the President when no candidate wins a majority. The House chose **John Quincy Adams**.

Andrew Jackson's supporters were furious. They believed the House should have chosen him as President.

The Election of 1828

In 1828, Andrew Jackson again ran for President, with John Quincy Adams as his only opponent. By that year, the Democratic-Republican Party had split into several groups. The group supporting Jackson became known as the **Democratic Party**—still one of our two major parties today.

The Democrats believed that wealthy businessmen and merchants would support Adams. But they believed Jackson could win the election if the common people supported him.

Crowds cheered Andrew Jackson on his way to Washington, D.C. This drawing appeared in *Harper's Weekly* in 1881.

The People's President

The Democrats came up with a new kind of campaign to win the support of the common people. In the past, campaigns had been fought mainly in the newspapers. Supporters had written articles about their candidates for voters to read. But many common people did not read newspapers. So, the Democrats held parades, barbecues, and dinners to stir up support for Jackson.

The new kind of campaign worked. In 1828, Jackson easily beat Adams.

Jackson's supporters saw his victory as a victory for the common people. Other Presidents had come from the East and were usually from wealthy families. But Andrew Jackson had grown up on the frontier. He had been poor as a boy. He had taught himself law and become a lawyer. He was the hero of the Battle of New Orleans, but Americans thought of him as one of the common people. To many, he was truly the ''people's President.''

Looking Back

1. Why did the House of Representatives choose the President in 1824?
2. What new kind of campaign did the Democrats use to win the common people's support for Andrew Jackson?
3. Why was Andrew Jackson thought of as the ''people's President''?

Chapter 10

Review

Facts First

Use words below to complete each sentence.

Andrew Jackson   Missouri Compromise
cotton gin   neutral
Democratic Party   textile mills
identical parts   Treaty of Ghent
Industrial Revolution   War Hawks

1. During the _____, factories began to be built in the United States.
2. Some of the first American factories were _____.
3. Eli Whitney's _____ helped to make cotton ''king'' in the South.
4. Whitney's idea for _____ made the mass production of goods possible.
5. America tried to remain _____ during Britain's war with France.
6. _____ wanted war with Britain to protect free trade and sailors' rights.
7. The _____ ended the War of 1812.
8. The _____ ended a disagreement over slavery in the Louisiana Territory.
9. In 1828, the _____ campaigned to win the support of the common people.
10. _____ was known as the ''people's President.''

Word Check

Write the meaning of each of these words. Then use each word in a sentence.

factory   produce
invent   section

Skill Builder

These items used to be made by hand at home. Today, most of these items are made by machines in factories. Give a report on how Americans used to make one of the items below. Look for the information in library books, or interview someone who knows.

baskets   furniture   quilts
cloth   nails   smoked ham
dyes   paper   soap

Chapter 10 Notes

Read over the chapter. Find answers to these questions:

1. How did factories change America?
2. How did the cotton gin change the South?
3. How did Eli Whitney's system of identical parts change the way things were made?
4. What problems with Britain on the sea and on the frontier led to the War of 1812?
5. How did people in the North and South disagree about slavery?
6. How did the Missouri Compromise satisfy both the slave and the free states?
7. What was new about the Democratic campaign to elect Andrew Jackson President in 1828?

Be a Historian

Historians learn about the past from letters and diaries that people wrote. Pictures and photographs people saved show us how they lived. What writings, drawings, and photographs could describe *your* life to other people? Gather some of those things. Make a poster about your life.

Chapter 11 From Sea to Shining Sea

Mr. Dougherty's Agency on the Missouri River kept supplies for traders, hunters, and Plains people. This engraving was printed in Europe.

Andrew Jackson's presidency ended in 1837. Five Presidents served after him during the 1840s. They were Martin Van Buren, William Henry Harrison, John Tyler, James Polk, and Zachary Taylor.

When Andrew Jackson was President, Americans wanted the country to expand westward, all the way to the Pacific Ocean. By the time Zachary Taylor was President, in 1849, Texas, Oregon, California, and New Mexico had become United States land. The nation *had expanded*—it now stretched "from sea to shining sea."

- How did Texas win its independence from Mexico?
- How did Oregon become part of the United States?
- Why did California grow rapidly in 1849?

Key Words You will be using these words in this chapter. Look them up in the glossary at the back of Part 1.

annex	boundary
border	expansion

Americans Settle in Texas

For years, Texas and Mexico were part of New Spain, the Spanish territory in North America. In 1821, Mexico won its independence from Spain, and Texas became part of the nation of Mexico.

An American, **Moses Austin**, asked Mexico for permission to start a colony in Texas. The Mexican government agreed, and American families began settling in the Austin colony.

Other Americans also asked for and received permission from Mexico to settle in Texas. Texas was a land of opportunity to them. Cotton grew well there, and many settlers began cotton plantations. Others started cattle ranches on the grasslands. Soon, thousands of Americans were coming to Texas.

By 1832, there were about 30,000 Americans in Texas. Many were not happy under Mexican rule. Mexico expected them to become Catholics. It also did not want them to own slaves. But many of the Americans had come from the South. They believed they had the right to own slaves.

The Americans Rebel Against Mexico

The Mexican government feared that Texas was becoming more American than Mexican. In 1830, the government tried to stop American settlers from moving into Texas. Mexican troops were sent to tighten Mexico's control over Texas. Those actions angered the Americans. In 1835, they revolted against the Mexican government.

Looking Back
1. How did Americans begin settling in Texas?
2. Why were the Americans unhappy under Mexican rule?

Sam Houston led Texans to independence. The U.S. postage stamps (*left and far right*) honor Houston and Texas statehood. The painting (*middle*) hangs in the San Jacinto Museum of History, La Porte, Texas.

Courtesy, Archives Division, Texas State Library

The Texas Revolution

Texas leaders met at the Austin colony. They set up their own government for Texas. Texan troops then attacked the town of San Antonio and drove out the Mexican troops.

General **Antonio Lopez de Santa Anna** marched from Mexico with an army of about 4000 troops. He planned to crush the revolution. In February 1836, the army reached San Antonio.

Fewer than 200 American fighters were in San Antonio. They withdrew behind the walls of an old mission called the **Alamo** and turned it into a fort.

Santa Anna's army surrounded the Alamo. For 12 days, the Mexicans attacked the Americans. But the outnumbered rebels would not surrender. Time after time, the Americans drove the Mexicans back. Finally, on March 6, the Mexicans overran the Alamo. All of the American fighters were killed.

"Remember the Alamo"

During the battle of the Alamo, Texas leaders met again. On March 2, they declared that Texas was independent from Mexico. They chose a commander for the Texas army, **Sam Houston**.

When Texans heard the news of the slaughter at the Alamo, they were enraged. They now had a battle cry in their fight for independence—"Remember the Alamo!"

Victory at San Jacinto

For the next month or so, Santa Anna's army moved through Texas. Sam Houston and the smaller Texas army retreated before the Mexicans.

Then, on April 21, Houston's army suddenly attacked the Mexicans near the San Jacinto River. The Mexicans were caught completely by surprise. In 18 minutes, the Battle of San Jacinto was over. Nearly all of Santa Anna's troops were killed or captured. Texas had won its independence from Mexico.

The Republic of Texas

The new Texas government set up the **Republic of Texas**. Like the United States, Texas would be governed by elected leaders. In 1836, Texans elected Sam Houston their first president. Texans also voted to join the United States.

But President Andrew Jackson did not want to *annex* Texas to the Union. He feared such an action would lead to war with Mexico. Many northerners also opposed annexing Texas because Texas would be a slave state. Texas remained an independent republic for nearly ten years.

Looking Back

1. How was the government of Texas organized after independence?
2. Why didn't Texas become a state in 1836?

Americans Move to Oregon

By 1840, American settlement had expanded to the Great Plains. There it stopped. Settlers believed the Great Plains were too dry for farming.

Then, in the early 1840s, Americans began to hear news from the Oregon region, far away on the Pacific coast. Americans heard that the Oregon region was a land of tall trees, rich soil, and fish-filled streams. Thousands of Americans decided to move there.

The Oregon Trail

Many settlers traveled to the Oregon region by a route called the **Oregon Trail**. The Oregon Trail began in Independence, Missouri. It crossed the Great Plains, then went over the Rocky Mountains, in present-day Wyoming. The trail then followed the Columbia River into the Oregon region. The journey covered about 2000 miles. Settlers had to travel four to six months to make it.

Most settlers traveled by *wagon train*— a group of covered wagons that traveled together. Wagon trains traveled 10 to 15 miles a day on the Plains. Travel was slower in the mountains and across rivers. It might take settlers a week to cross a fast-flowing river.

A wagon train travels over the Oregon Trail.

Library of Congress

The United States and Britain Both Claim Oregon

Thousands of Americans settled in Oregon. Soon, a *dispute* (argument) arose between Britain and the United States. At that time, the Oregon region stretched from the Rockies to the Pacific Ocean and from California to Alaska. Both the United States and Britain claimed the region. They could not agree on a **boundary** between their territories.

In 1818, the United States and Britain had agreed that people from both nations could settle in the Oregon region. But by 1843, American settlers there greatly outnumbered British settlers. The Americans asked Congress to make Oregon a territory of the United States.

The Oregon Treaty

In the election year of 1844, **James Polk** was a candidate for President. He claimed that the whole area of the Oregon region belonged to the United States, not Britain. He said that the United States should take that area by force if necessary. Most Americans agreed with Polk. He was elected President.

In 1846, President Polk reached an agreement with Britain. That agreement was called the **Oregon Treaty**. The treaty divided the Oregon region between Britain and the United States. Britain received the northern part, or land that is now western Canada. The United States received the southern part, land that is now Washington, Oregon, Idaho, and parts of Wyoming and Montana.

Looking Back

1. What did the pioneers believe about the Great Plains?
2. How did pioneers get to Oregon?
3. How did the Oregon Treaty divide land between two countries?

The War with Mexico (1846-1848)

In 1845, Americans began to move south into Texas and west into California. You remember that Texas was an independent republic. California was now part of Mexico, which had won independence from Spain in 1821.

American *expansion* again led to a dispute—this time with Mexico.

The Annexation of Texas

Texas had first asked to join the United States in 1836, the year that Texas won its independence from Mexico. In 1845, Congress finally annexed Texas, and Texas became the 28th state.

The annexation of Texas quickly led to trouble with Mexico. Mexico and the United States disagreed about the southern *border* of Texas. The United States claimed that the border was the Rio Grande River. Mexico claimed the border was along the Nueces River, farther north.

In 1845, President Polk sent John Slidell to Mexico to talk to Mexican government officials. Slidell had two assignments from President Polk: first, to settle the dispute over the Texas border, and second, to offer to buy California and New Mexico from Mexico.

This U.S. postage stamp honors the Battle of the Alamo.

Americans Want California

President Polk believed California should be added to the United States for two reasons: First, hundreds of American citizens had settled in California by 1845. Second, California had excellent harbors, especially San Francisco Bay. Those harbors could provide good stopping places for American ships going to Asia.

But Mexico did not want to lose California. And the Mexican government was angry over the annexation of Texas and the border dispute. When John Slidell arrived in Mexico, Mexican government officials refused to see him.

War Begins

In 1846, President Polk sent troops to Texas. General **Zachary Taylor** was in charge of those troops. Taylor's troops camped on land along the Rio Grande River—land that the United States claimed.

But Mexico also claimed that land. A Mexican army moved north and camped across the river from the Americans. On April 25, the Mexicans attacked Taylor's troops.

President Polk called for war. Mexico "has invaded our territory and shed American blood upon American soil," he said. In May, Congress declared war.

Many Americans opposed the war. One was a young Congressman from Illinois. His name was **Abraham Lincoln**. Lincoln believed that Mexico had a rightful claim to the land along the Rio Grande.

Looking Back

1. How did the annexation of Texas lead to war with Mexico?
2. Why did the United States want California?
3. Why did Abraham Lincoln oppose war with Mexico?

THE UNITED STATES 1848 AND TODAY

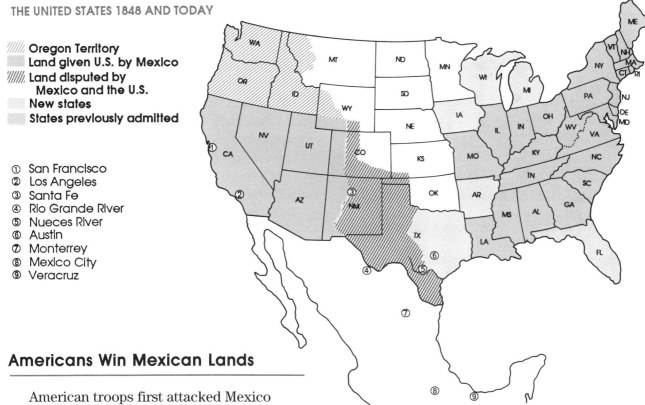

Oregon Territory
Land given U.S. by Mexico
Land disputed by
    Mexico and the U.S.
New states
States previously admitted

① San Francisco
② Los Angeles
③ Santa Fe
④ Rio Grande River
⑤ Nueces River
⑥ Austin
⑦ Monterrey
⑧ Mexico City
⑨ Veracruz

Americans Win Mexican Lands

American troops first attacked Mexico along its northern borders. Led by Zachary Taylor, the Americans won a series of battles. By the end of 1846, they had captured the city of Monterrey in northern Mexico.

Meanwhile, an American army under General Stephen Kearny invaded Mexican territory in the American Southwest. The Americans captured Santa Fe, in New Mexico, and marched west into California. In January 1847, the Americans captured Los Angeles.

American Victories

The United States also sent troops by ship to the southern part of Mexico. The ships landed in the town of Veracruz. The American army, led by General Winfield Scott, fought its way from Veracruz to Mexico City, the capital of Mexico. Mexican troops fought bravely to defend their capital. On September 14, 1847, Mexico City fell to the Americans.

The Treaty of Guadalupe Hidalgo

In early 1848, Mexico and the United States signed a peace treaty at the Mexican town of **Guadalupe Hidalgo**. Mexico agreed that the Rio Grande was the southern border of Texas. And Mexico gave up California and New Mexico territory. (New Mexico territory would later become New Mexico, Arizona, Utah, and Nevada.)

In exchange, the United States paid Mexico $15 million and promised to treat Mexicans living in its new territory as American citizens.

Looking Back

1. What territory did the United States gain in the Mexican War?
2. What did Mexico get from the United States?
3. *Map work*: What states today have land that Mexico gave up in 1848?

This engraving shows "actual life at the mines."

The Gold Rush

"GOLD, GOLD, GOLD IN CALIFORNIA!" Those words were in newspaper headlines throughout the nation in 1848. Gold had been discovered in the foothills of California's mountain range, the Sierra Nevada.

By 1849, thousands of people from around the world were rushing to California. That "rush" for California gold became known as the **gold rush**.

California Here I Come

The people who came to California in 1849 were called *forty-niners*. Thousands of forty-niners came by ship. They came from the east coast of the United States, from Mexico, South America, Europe, Australia, and China. Thousands of others traveled overland to California. In 1849 alone, about 80,000 people came to California.

Many forty-niners rushed to the mountains to look for gold. But others stayed in towns to open stores and businesses. Quiet settlements, such as San Francisco and Sacramento, suddenly became fast-growing towns. During the year of 1849, San Francisco's population grew from less than 1000 to 25,000.

The Mining Camps

Many *prospectors*, or gold-seekers, lived in mining camps with names such as *Rough and Ready* and *Skunk Gulch*. Some prospectors did find gold in the gravel bottoms of streams and rivers. But they did not have the tools to dig deep mines. And most of the gold was buried deep in the mountains, out of the prospectors' reach.

Life in the camps was hard. Food and supplies were costly. Merchants and saloon-keepers got rich selling sugar for $4 a pound and whiskey for $20 a bottle.

There was little law and order. Thieves robbed the prospectors of their gold. Gamblers cheated them. Beatings and murders were common.

To protect themselves, prospectors sometimes caught and punished criminals themselves. They formed groups and called themselves *vigilantes*. Anyone caught by the vigilantes was quickly hanged, often without a trial. One camp changed its name to Hangtown to warn away thieves.

California Becomes a State

By 1850, there were enough people in California for it to become the nation's 31st state.

Many of the gold-seekers stayed in the new state. Some started businesses. Others became farmers. They discovered that California had some of the richest farmland in the nation.

Looking Back

1. What was the California gold rush?
2. How did it affect the growth of California?
3. What was life like in the mining camps?
4. Today, California has more people than any other state. Why do you think that is so?

Chapter 11  Review

Facts First

Complete each sentence by choosing the correct ending.

1. Before Texas became independent, it was controlled by
   a. Great Britain.
   b. the United States.
   c. Mexico.
2. Texas won its independence and
   a. became a part of California.
   b. became a republic.
   c. became part of Mexico.
3. Most pioneers traveled to Oregon by
   a. ship.
   b. train.
   c. wagon train.
4. The U.S. gained control of Oregon by
   a. going to war with Britain.
   b. a peaceful settlement with Britain.
   c. buying Oregon from Mexico.
5. The Mexican War began when
   a. American and Mexican troops fought over land that both countries claimed.
   b. Americans started colonies in Mexico.
   c. forty-niners poured into California.
6. The treaty ending the Mexican War gave the U.S.
   a. Mexico.
   b. California and New Mexico territory.
   c. Oregon.
7. The California gold rush
   a. made every gold-seeker rich.
   b. slowed the growth of California.
   c. brought rapid growth to California.

Word Check

Write the meaning of each of these words. Then use each word in a sentence.

annex	boundary
border	expansion

Skill Builder

Find out in what years these events happened. Then write them in order.

- California becomes a state.
- Americans first settle in Texas.
- The Alamo falls.
- The California gold rush begins.
- The Mexican War ends.
- The U.S. annexes Texas.
- Texas wins its independence.

Chapter 11 Notes

Read over the chapter. Find answers to these questions:

1. How did Texas become an independent republic?
2. Why did the U.S. and Britain argue over Oregon territory? How did they settle the argument?
3. What did the U.S. gain from the Mexican War?
4. How did the gold rush change California?

Be a Historian

In the 1840s, thousands of people immigrated to the United States. Most of those immigrants came from Ireland, Germany, and other European nations.

Where do you think most American immigrants come from today? Check an almanac or encyclopedia to find out.

Bonus

Find out about one of these important people from America's past. Then report what you learned.

Stephen Austin	John Sutter
James Bowie	Zachary Taylor
John C. Fremont	Narcissa Whitman
Sam Houston	Brigham Young
James Polk	

Chapter 12 **Changing Ways of Life**

Woolaroc Museum, Bartlesville, Oklahoma

The years from 1800 to 1850 saw great changes in American life. In 1800, most Americans lived near the Atlantic coast. By 1850, Americans were settling along the Pacific coast.

New inventions changed the way Americans traveled and carried on business. Cities grew rapidly.

For many, America continued to be a land of great opportunity. But for other Americans, life in America was hard. Change and growth brought problems and hardship.

- Why were Indians in the East forced to leave their homelands?
- How did Americans help improve the lives of others?
- What new inventions changed the ways Americans traveled and shipped goods?
- What problems did America's growing cities face?

Key Words   You will be using these words in this chapter. Look them up in the glossary at the back of Part 1.

communicate	**reservation**
reformer	**transportation**

One-fourth of the Cherokee people died when they were forced to move from Georgia to the Indian Territory in 1838. They called their unhappy journey the Trail of Tears. This scene is from a Robert Lindneux painting.

Conflict with Native Americans

You read that the first English settlements were on the east coast of America. At first, the Indians there were friendly to settlers. But as more settlers arrived, conflicts developed between the settlers and the Indians.

The eastern lands were thickly covered with forests. Those forests were home to the Indians. The forests provided them with everything they needed to live. But settlers saw the forests as useless wilderness. They cleared the forests and turned them into farmland. Indians soon learned that when forests became farmland, deer and other game disappeared.

During the 1600s and 1700s, Indians often fought to keep settlers off their lands. But the settlers kept arriving, and they had better weapons than the Indians. As more settlers moved onto Indian lands, the Indians were pushed farther and farther west.

After independence, the United States government made treaties with the Indians. In those treaties, the Indians gave up much of their land. In return, certain lands in the Northwest Territory and the South were *reserved* just for Indians. Those lands were called Indian **reservations**.

The government promised to protect the Indians and keep settlers off their reserved lands. But those promises were broken. Settlers moved onto Indian land. And the Indians went to war against the settlers.

Indian Removal

When Andrew Jackson became President in 1829, he wanted to end the conflict with the Indians. Jackson believed there could be no peace on the frontier while any Indians lived east of the Mississippi. He insisted that all eastern Indians be moved west.

In 1830, Congress passed the **Indian Removal Act**. That law gave the President power to make treaties with the Indians in order to move them. The treaties were agreements between the United States and the different Indian peoples: The United States would pay the Indians a certain amount of money for their lands, and the Indians would move to reservations in present-day Kansas and Oklahoma. Those lands were called **Indian Territory**.

The Northern Indians

Most Indian peoples in the North signed removal treaties. Some were tricked into signing, and some were forced to sign by bands of armed frontier settlers.

In 1832, Sauk and Fox Indians in Illinois rebelled against the removal. They were led by Chief **Black Hawk**. The uprising became known as the **Black Hawk War**. Federal troops hunted down Black Hawk and his followers. The Indians saw they were trapped and waved a white flag to show that they surrendered. But the troops attacked anyway and killed all but a few of the Sauks.

The Southern Indians

Five Indian peoples lived in the South. The Choctaw of Mississippi were the first of the five to leave their homeland for Indian Territory. The Chickasaw and Creek were the next to leave. Nearly half the Creek died on the long journey to Indian Territory or in their first year there.

INDIAN REMOVAL 1830 - 1842

① Choctaw
② Chickasaw
③ Creek
④ Cherokee
⑤ Seminole
■ Indian Territory

The Seminoles in Florida refused to leave their lands. For seven years, they fought federal troops in the swamps of Florida, from 1835 to 1842. That was the longest Indian war. Finally, most of the Seminoles were driven west.

The Cherokee of Georgia also fought removal. The Cherokee did not want to leave their farms and villages. They had adopted many of the ways of the settlers. A Cherokee named Sequoyah had created a written language for his people. The Cherokee printed a weekly newspaper in both Cherokee and English.

The Trail of Tears

The Cherokee asked the federal courts to protect their rights and their land. In 1832, the Supreme Court ruled that the Cherokee should be left alone. President Jackson and Georgia settlers ignored the Court. They wanted Cherokee land.

The Cherokee were forced to leave Georgia in 1838. Those who tried to stay were dragged from their homes and loaded into wagons. On the long journey to Indian Territory, a fourth of the Cherokee died. The survivors would always remember their route west as the **Trail of Tears**.

Looking Back
1. Why did Indians and settlers come into conflict?
2. What did the Indian Removal Act do?
3. Why did President Jackson ignore the Supreme Court ruling?
4. *Map work:* What was the route of the "Trail of Tears"?

Reformers Work to Change America

During the 1830s and 1840s, the United States was beginning to develop widespread *social problems*—problems that have to do with the ways people work and live. Too many Americans were poor or ill. Too many did not have the same rights or opportunities as others. ***Reformers*** began to try to improve the lives of those Americans.

The Religious Revival

Many of the reformers were religious people. Religion had always been important to Americans. By the 1800s, thousands of churches could be found throughout the nation.

During the 1830s and 1840s, Christian ministers held meetings to *revive*, or wake up, religious feelings. At those *revival meetings*, ministers spoke to huge crowds. The ministers urged people to begin leading better lives. They also urged people to help others.

The Temperance Movement

A widespread problem in the 1800s was *alcoholism*—a disease in which a person cannot control his or her drinking of alcohol. Alcoholism led to problems such as poor health, loss of jobs, poverty, and crime.

Reformers urged Americans to *temper*, or control, their drinking. They set up groups called *temperance societies*. At temperance meetings, speakers asked people to take "the pledge." That was a promise not to drink any liquor.

The **temperance movement** spread throughout the nation. Thirteen states passed laws to stop the sale of alcohol, but those laws were hard to enforce. Within a few years, most of those laws were repealed.

Thomas Gallaudet

Library of Congress

The monument at right honors Thomas Gallaudet, who set up a school for deaf children.

Helping the Helpless

Other reformers helped people who were sick or disabled. **Dorothea Dix** helped people who were mentally ill. She was shocked by the way mentally ill people were treated. They were locked up in unheated prisons. When they caused trouble, they were beaten.

Dorothea Dix wrote about what she saw. She urged that the mentally ill be treated as sick people, not as criminals. She went from state to state, speaking to lawmakers. Because of her work, 15 states built hospitals for the mentally ill.

Schools for the Disabled

Reformers also worked to help the deaf and blind. In Connecticut, **Thomas Gallaudet** set up a school for deaf children. He taught his students to read, write, and ***communicate*** with others. Soon, other schools were using his methods.

Samuel Howe headed a school for the blind in Massachusetts. He taught his students to read *Braille*, a writing system in which letters are made with small raised dots. Students feel the dots and "read" the letters with their fingers. Howe also taught his students how to get around by themselves and take care of themselves.

Looking Back

1. How did the religious revival movement help the reform movement to develop?
2. What was the temperance movement?
3. What reforms were begun to help the disabled?

Elizabeth Stanton

Lucretia Mott

Lucy Stone

Sojourner Truth

In the 1800s, these women worked for civil rights for women.   Library of Congress

The Women's Movement

Many of the most active reformers were women. As women worked to help others, they began to think about their own lack of rights.

In the 1830s, women could not vote or hold office. Most women could not own property. Women did not attend high schools or colleges. They could not become doctors or lawyers or hold many other jobs.

Most men believed that women belonged at home, and that they should spend their lives caring for their husbands and children. If a woman did hold a job, her husband controlled the money that she made. Wife-beating was legal in most states.

Women Reformers Speak Out

Women such as **Margaret Fuller** began to speak out about the rights of women. Margaret Fuller was a newspaper reporter, the first American woman to have such a job. She argued that women should be able to work in any job. ''Let them be sea-captains, if you will,'' she wrote.

Elizabeth Stanton and **Lucretia Mott** became leaders in the fight for women's rights. In 1848, Stanton and Mott held the world's first women's rights convention at Seneca Falls, New York. About 300 women and men attended the convention.

The Declaration of Sentiments

The delegates adopted a **Declaration of Sentiments** that called for equal rights for women, including the right to vote. The Declaration of Sentiments began like the Declaration of Independence, with one important change. It said: ''We hold these truths to be self-evident: that all men *and women* are created equal.''

The delegates demanded full legal rights for women. They also asked for equal education and job opportunities.

At first, men made fun of women's demands. Since men controlled the legislatures, changes were slow in coming. But women continued to fight for their rights. More than 70 years after the Seneca Falls convention, women won the right to vote throughout the country.

Looking Back
1. What were some rights women did not have in the 1830s?
2. What rights did women call for in the Declaration of Sentiments?
3. What problems in America today would you like to solve? Why?

Travel Becomes Easier

Between 1800 and 1850, new forms of *transportation* developed rapidly in the United States.

Turnpikes Make Land Travel Easier

Most roads in America were badly made. Then private companies began building better roads. The roads were called *macadam roads*. Macadam roads were shaped so that water ran off them. They were also *paved*, or covered, with a thick layer of small stones that made them smooth.

People who wanted to use the roads paid a fee to the companies that built them. Those roads became known as *turnpikes*.

Canals Make New Water Routes

Americans also used rivers for transportation. They could travel long distances faster by boat than by wagon on land. But rivers did not connect all parts of the country with each other. So, Americans began to build long *canals*. A canal is a deep waterway that people make by digging across an area of land. The first long canal to be dug was the **Erie Canal**. It opened in 1825 and was 363 miles long. The Erie Canal linked the Hudson River near Albany, New York, to Lake Erie near Buffalo, New York.

The Erie Canal was a great success. Ships could travel from Albany to Lake Erie in eight days. On land, the same journey took 20 days. The cost of shipping goods from Lake Erie to the East fell from $100 a ton to less than $10. The Great Lakes became an important route for shipping farm crops to the east coast. Soon other canals opened in the East and Midwest.

Steamboats Make Water Travel Faster

In 1807, **Robert Fulton** put a **steam engine** on a boat. That was an engine that was powered by steam. It provided the energy to move the boat.

Fulton ran his first "steamboat" up the Hudson River in New York. Crowds of people watched from the banks of the river. They laughed at the boat and called it "Fulton's Folly"—Fulton's foolish mistake. But the steamboat traveled the 150 miles from New York City to Albany in just 32 hours. It usually took a ship with sails a week to make the same trip.

Americans quickly discovered that the steamboat was a reliable and fast way to travel and ship goods. By the 1830s, hundreds of steamboats had been built. They traveled on the Mississippi, the Ohio, and other rivers.

Railroads Make Land Travel Faster

During the early 1800s, an English inventor named **Richard Trevithick** put a steam engine onto a four-wheeled cart that ran on a track. It was the world's first railroad locomotive.

Then, in 1825, an American named **John Stevens** built the first American steam locomotive. In 1830, **Peter Cooper**, another American, built a locomotive that could pull 40 people at ten miles an hour. In a few years, railroad trains were being built that moved faster than sailboats, steamboats, or wagons. By 1850, thousands of miles of railroad tracks had been built east of the Mississippi River.

Looking Back

1. How did turnpikes improve transportation?
2. How did canals make faster routes for shipping goods to markets?
3. How did the steam engine improve transportation on the water? on land?

Library of Congress

Early steamboats and steam locomotives gave people a reliable and fast way to travel and to ship goods.

More Inventions Change American Life

New inventions also changed the ways Americans communicated, farmed, and worked between 1800 and 1850.

The Telegraph Makes Communication Faster

Before the 1830s, it took weeks and months for news to travel over the vast distances of America.

In 1837, **Samuel Morse** invented the *telegraph*. It was a way to send signals over wires using electricity. Using a code invented by Morse, people could tap out messages and send them over long distances. By 1851, telegraph wires were strung as far west as St. Louis, Missouri. By 1862, the wires reached the Pacific.

The Reaper Changes Farming

New inventions also changed farm life. In the past, almost all farm jobs had been done by hand. For example, people had planted, weeded, and harvested their crops by hand.

In 1834, **Cyrus McCormick** invented a mechanical *reaper* to harvest grain. It was a large machine, something like a giant lawn mower, that was pulled by horses. Its sharp blades cut the grain as it moved through a field. Farmers using a reaper could harvest as much wheat in a day as they had in a week cutting by hand.

Inventions for the Home

Other inventions changed life at home. In 1839, **Charles Goodyear** invented a way to make things with rubber. Soon, Americans were buying rubber boots, raincoats, hats, and buckets.

Elias Howe invented a sewing machine in 1846. Before then, clothes had been sewn by hand. The machine did as much in an hour as a hand sewer did in a day.

Americans learned about new inventions in their newspapers. Newspapers had once been too expensive for most people. Then inventors found ways to make cheap paper and faster printing presses. The price of a newspaper dropped to a penny.

Looking Back
1. How did the telegraph improve communication?
2. How did the reaper and sewing machine change work that was once done by hand?
3. Which of the inventions that you read about are still being used today?

The Growing Cities

Between 1800 and 1850, the nation's cities grew rapidly. With rapid growth came many problems.

Immigrants Face Hard Life in Cities

In the first half of the 1800s, thousands of immigrants came to the United States. The largest groups came from Ireland, Germany, Britain, and France.

Many immigrants headed west, looking for land to farm. But many others stayed in the eastern cities. They found work in factories. Factory work was hard: Workers worked long hours at low pay.

The cities did not have enough housing for the newcomers. Poor families often lived in *tenements*—apartment buildings in which families were crowded into tiny rooms. The tenements were dirty and run-down.

City Problems: Lack of Services

Today, city governments provide many services, such as police and fire protection and garbage collection. But those *city services* did not exist in the early 1800s.

Cities did not have trained fire fighters. Fires were fought by unpaid volunteers. Most city buildings were made of wood and were built close together. Fires started easily and spread quickly.

Cities had no police protection. Gangs roamed the streets. Robberies and stabbings were common.

Sanitation in the cities was poor. Garbage was dumped in the streets. Much of it was eaten by wandering herds of pigs and goats. The rest of the garbage was left to rot. As a result, most cities smelled bad. And germs spread disease. Every few years, smallpox or some other disease killed thousands of city people.

This woodcut shows a city wharf on fire in 1820.

Library of Congress

Many cities did not have safe drinking water. Water came from backyard wells or was sold from door to door out of wooden tubs. By 1844, New York City had built a *reservoir*, or lake, 40 miles away. Water was brought to the city through a tunnel about eight feet in diameter. For the first time, New Yorkers had running water.

Cities Provide Entertainment

Despite their many problems, cities were exciting places to live in or visit. Plays and musical events were put on in opera houses and music halls. There were museums that held anything from ancient animal bones to wax figures of famous people.

Shopping was another form of city entertainment. In 1846, a huge store opened in New York with a new look. It used display windows to show off its goods. Window-shopping became a new American pastime.

Looking Back

1. In what parts of America did most immigrants settle between 1800 and 1850?
2. What were city tenements like?
3. Why were fires a serious problem in cities?
4. Why was sanitation poor in the cities?
5. What are some problems of cities today?

Chapter 12

Review

Facts First

Complete each sentence by choosing the correct ending.

1. During the 1700s and 1800s, settlers
   a. stayed off Indian land.
   b. pushed the Indians farther west.
   c. seldom fought with the Indians.
2. The Indian Removal Act
   a. forced Indians onto reservations.
   b. allowed Indians to stay in the East.
   c. was popular with the Cherokee.
3. Temperance speakers urged people to
   a. control their tempers.
   b. move west.
   c. give up alcohol.
4. Dorothea Dix urged states to
   a. put the mentally ill in jail.
   b. build hospitals for the mentally ill.
   c. teach Braille to the mentally ill.
5. In the 1830s, women could not
   a. be reformers.
   b. attend church.
   c. vote or hold office.
6. The women's rights movement of the 1840s
   a. won women the right to vote.
   b. was led mainly by men.
   c. demanded full legal rights for women.
7. Turnpikes, steamboats, and canals
   a. improved transportation in the U.S.
   b. never caught on in America.
   c. were used mainly in New York.
8. Most cities in the early 1800s
   a. had no city services.
   b. were clean.
   c. had safe drinking water.

Word Check

Write the meaning of each of these words. Then use each word in a sentence.

communicate   **reservation**
reformer   **transportation**

Skill Builder

Between 1800 and 1850, 15 states were added to the Union. Find the states listed below on a map of the United States. Then make your own map showing *all* the states in the country by 1850.

Ohio (1803)   Arkansas (1836)
Louisiana (1812)   Michigan (1837)
Indiana (1816)   Florida (1845)
Mississippi (1817)   Texas (1845)
Illinois (1818)   Iowa (1846)
Alabama (1819)   Wisconsin (1848)
Maine (1820)   California (1850)
Missouri (1821)

Chapter 12 Notes

Read over the chapter. Find answers to these questions:

1. What was the Trail of Tears? Why was it given that name?
2. How did these people try to improve life for others?
   a. Thomas Gallaudet
   b. Samuel Howe
   c. Elizabeth Stanton
3. How was transportation on land made faster and easier in the early 1800s?
4. What inventions made travel by water faster and easier?
5. What was it like to live in an American city in the early 1800s?

Be a Historian

Below are several modern inventions. Find out more about one of them: Talk to people who have used the invention. Ask how the invention has changed their lives or work. Then report what you learned.

- personal stereos with headphones
- video cassette players (VCRs)
- personal computers
- microwave ovens
- telephone answering machines

Unit 4

Review

What Do You Know?

Complete each sentence by choosing the correct ending.

1. In 1800, France and Spain controlled
   a. no land in North America.
   b. land west of the Mississippi River.
   c. Virginia.
2. The Louisiana Purchase made the U.S.
   a. angry at Napoleon.
   b. change its Constitution.
   c. twice as large as it had been.
3. The Industrial Revolution was the
   a. revolt of unhappy factory workers.
   b. shift of work from home to factory.
   c. event that made Texas independent.
4. Andrew Jackson was called the "people's President" because
   a. men, women, and children voted for him.
   b. he was one of the "common people."
   c. he was the first elected president.
5. In 1846, the U.S. and Mexico fought over
   a. fishing waters both countries wanted.
   b. land that both countries claimed.
   c. the Oregon region.
6. In the Mexican War, the U.S. won
   a. the Louisiana Territory.
   b. Oregon territory.
   c. California and New Mexico.
7. The Indian Removal Act
   a. helped Indians keep their homes.
   b. forced Indians from their homes.
   c. allowed Indians to go to Oregon.
8. New inventions in the 1800s
   a. made travel more expensive.
   b. brought steam power to land and river travel.
   c. made travel less comfortable.

What Do You Think?

Travel has changed greatly in America since 1840.

1. How is travel today different from travel in the 1840s?
2. How do you think Americans will be traveling in the future?

Skill Builder

Below are some American inventors of the 1800s. Find out what these inventors invented. (Look in an encyclopedia or history book.)

Samuel Colt	Elias Howe
John Deere	Walter Hunt
Charles Goodyear	Crawford Long
John Gorrie	Cyrus McCormick
Richard Hoe	Charles Otis

Unit 4 Notes

Look over the unit to find answers to these questions:

1. How did the U.S. grow larger and richer from the Louisiana Purchase?
2. How did new machines and factories change American life?
3. What is sectionalism? What did people in the North and South disagree about?
4. Why did the U.S. go to war against Britain in 1812? against Mexico in 1846?
5. How did the U.S. get Indians off land that American settlers wanted?
6. How did inventions change the way people traveled in the early 1800s?

Word Builder

Write a story about what happened to American Indians in the 1800s. Use all the key words listed below.

Key Words

communicate	frontier	reservation
expansion	pioneer	section

The Nation Divided

Maryland—1852

Two men on horses gallop along a country road. They stop to nail a sheet of paper onto a tree. The paper describes Harriet Tubman. She is an African American, about five feet tall. There are scars on her back and forehead. She is wanted for the crime of stealing slaves.

The men ride on. A small African American woman steps out of the woods onto the road. She is followed by nine runaway slaves. One of them reads the paper aloud. Harriet Tubman listens and then rips down the sheet.

Harriet Tubman leads the runaways back into the woods. As they walk through the trees, she talks about her life. She describes the Maryland farm where she was born into slavery. She talks about the owners who left the scars on her back and forehead.

Then she tells the story of her escape. At first, she had traveled alone, with no guide but the North Star. Then she had discovered the *Underground Railroad.* It is not a real railroad, she explains. It is a group of people who help enslaved people escape from the South. They hide runaways by day in "waiting rooms"—their homes or barns. At night, they help runaways move on to the next "station." People in the Underground Railroad had helped Harriet Tubman reach the North.

Harriet Tubman leads the nine runaways to safety. Again and again, she returns to the South to help other runaways. She comes to be known as "Moses" Tubman. Like Moses in the Bible, she leads her people out of slavery.

In Our Time

Harriet Tubman lived in a troubled nation. Sections of the country had become very different from each other—with different ideas and ways of life. Arguments between sections had become more frequent and more serious.

Today, Americans still face difficult problems. But there are still people like Harriet Tubman. They are people who take action to improve the nation we live in. Who are some people today who are working to solve the nation's problems?

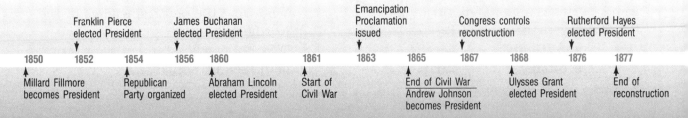

	Franklin Pierce elected President		James Buchanan elected President				Emancipation Proclamation issued		Congress controls reconstruction		Rutherford Hayes elected President	
1850	1852	1854	1856	1860		1861	1863	1865	1867	1868	1876	1877
Millard Fillmore becomes President		Republican Party organized		Abraham Lincoln elected President		Start of Civil War		End of Civil War / Andrew Johnson becomes President		Ulysses Grant elected President		End of reconstruction

Chapter 13 The Nation Pulls Apart

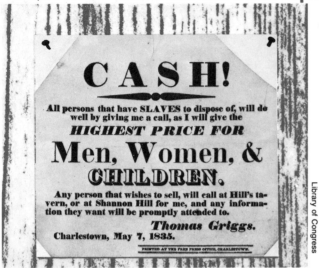

CASH!

All persons that have SLAVES to dispose of, will do well by giving me a call, as I will give the

HIGHEST PRICE FOR

Men, Women, & CHILDREN.

Any person that wishes to sell, will call at Hill's tavern, or at Shannon Hill for me, and any information they want will be promptly attended to.

Thomas Griggs.

Charlestown, May 7, 1835.

PRINTED AT THE FREE PRESS OFFICE, CHARLESTOWN.

Library of Congress

This is a poster from 1835.

In the first half of the 1800s, the nation was divided into three major sections. They were the Northeast, the Midwest, and the South. (The Midwest was the part of the country next to the Northeast.)

As you read in Chapter 10, sectionalism began to divide the nation in the 1820s. Each section of the country had its own way of life. People in different sections had different ideas about how the federal government should help the nation grow.

From time to time, differences among sections almost split the nation. After much arguing in Congress, a compromise was always found.

But during the 1850s, Americans found it hard to compromise on one issue—slavery.

- What was life like in different sections of the country?
- What was life like for a slave?
- How did differences over slavery finally pull the nation apart?

Key Words   You will be using these words in this chapter. Look them up in the glossary at the back of Part 1.

abolitionist   secede
economy   tariff

The Northeast: Land of Businesses

The Northeast was made up of states along the northeastern coast of the nation. Look at the map on page 93. What states were in the Northeast?

The Industrial Revolution had begun in the Northeast. There were more factories, stores, and banks there than in other parts of the country. Most of the nation's cloth and other factory-made goods were produced there.

The political leaders of the Northeast were business people. They wanted a strong national government. They believed a strong government could help business.

Northeasterners Want Tariffs

Northeasterners asked Congress for *tariffs*. A tariff is a tax on imported goods. The purpose of a tariff is to protect a business from foreign competition.

Tariffs helped American businesses by making foreign goods cost more. For example, when Congress placed a tariff on foreign cloth, the price of that cloth went up. Owners of American textile mills did not have to pay the tariff, so they could sell their cloth for less. People would then buy the less costly American cloth instead of the imported cloth.

During the 1850s, Congress helped businesses in the Northeast by placing tariffs on cloth, glass, iron, and other goods.

Looking Back
1. Who were the political leaders of the Northeast?
2. Why did northeasterners want tariffs to be passed by Congress?

MAJOR SECTIONS IN 1850
- Northeast
- Midwest
- South

The Midwest: Land of Small Farms

The Midwest was made up of the states around the Great Lakes. Look at the map. What were those states?

The Midwest was settled mainly by owners of small farms. Those farmers raised corn, wheat, cattle, pigs, and sheep.

Northeast and Midwest Need Each Other

The *economy* of the Midwest was closely tied to the economy of the Northeast: The Northeast depended on the Midwest for meat and grain. The Midwest depended on the Northeast for goods such as boots and guns. Many canals and railroad lines connected the two sections.

Like northeasterners, midwesterners wanted a strong national government. They wanted the government to build more roads, canals, and railroads in the Midwest. Better transportation would allow them to get their crops to markets in the Northeast.

Members of Congress from the Midwest and Northeast supported one another. Midwestern members voted for high tariffs. In exchange, northeastern members voted for better transportation. And members from both sections opposed slavery.

The Midwest and Northeast often looked like one huge section to southerners. They called that section "the North."

The South: Land of Farms and Plantations

The South was made up of the slave states. Look at the map. What were the southern states?

People in the South lived on farms and large plantations. Their most important crops were cotton, tobacco, rice, and sugar.

The southern economy was built on slavery. Enslaved people grew and harvested the crops that made money for southerners. In 1850, one-fourth of all southern families were slaveholders. Most had just one or two enslaved people. But planters might have from 30 to 1000 slaves working on their plantations.

The political leaders of the South were mainly planters. They feared a strong national government. They thought a strong government might end slavery.

In Congress, southerners and northerners often disagreed. Southerners opposed high tariffs because the South had few factories to protect. Southerners also opposed the building of more roads, canals, and railroads in the North. Such projects did not help southerners.

Most of all, southerners disagreed with northerners about slavery.

Looking Back
1. How did the Northeast and the Midwest depend on each other?
2. How did people in the South make a living?
3. What did southerners and northerners disagree about in Congress?

Left: This engraving from *Harper's Weekly* shows enslaved African Americans on a plantation. Right: Enslaved people were held and sold in this building.

Slavery

The issue that most divided North and South was slavery. By 1860, there were about four million enslaved people who lived in the South.

African Americans who escaped from slavery told about hard work, cruel treatment, pain—and a longing for freedom.

Living Conditions

Some enslaved people lived in cities or on small farms. But most of them lived on large plantations. Enslaved people were put to work early in life. Enslaved children as young as six years old worked in the fields, carrying water. They continued to work throughout their lives until they were too old to do so.

Enslaved people depended on their owners for food, clothing, and a place to live. The food was usually the same week after week. Their meals were usually made up of cornbread and bacon or salt pork. Some enslaved people were allowed to raise vegetables in small gardens. Others trapped raccoons or opossums for meat.

Clothes for enslaved people rarely fit. Men and women were given the same kind of shoes. They complained that their shoes made their feet burn and blister in the summer. In the winter, the shoes became stiff from the cold.

Daily Life

Most enslaved families lived in crowded one-room cabins, or "slave quarters." The cabins often had no windows. A bell woke people at four o'clock in the morning. Thirty minutes later, they were on their way to the fields. Another bell rang in the afternoon, signaling a short break for lunch. After lunch, the work began again and went on until it was too dark to see.

Men, women, and children worked in the fields together. Trees had to be cut and fields plowed. Crops had to be planted, weeded, and harvested.

After leaving the fields, enslaved people still had work to do. Animals were fed. Wood was chopped. Often, it was midnight before they ate their supper and lay down to sleep. All too soon, the morning bell rang again.

Not all enslaved people worked in the fields. Some were house servants. Others worked as carpenters or dressmakers. Whatever their work, most worked from dawn to darkness. Only on Sunday could they rest.

Looking Back

1. What were living conditions like for most enslaved people?
2. What daily schedule did most enslaved people have to follow?

Control Over Enslaved People

Throughout the early 1800s, the number of enslaved people in the South steadily rose. Slaveholders worried about slave uprisings. They took steps to control the enslaved people.

For example, it was against the law to teach enslaved people to read. If they were educated, they might read books and pamphlets that gave them ideas about freedom.

Enslaved people could not travel away from home without passes. They were told that they must obey any white person without asking questions. Those who did not learn to respect whites were whipped. A common punishment was 39 lashes with a cowhide whip. Few enslaved people reached old age without being whipped at least once.

Slaveholders also controlled the family life of enslaved people. Marriages were illegal. At any time, enslaved people could be taken from their families and sold. Children were sometimes taken away from their parents and sold, never to be seen by their families again.

Runaways and Rebels

Despite attempts to control enslaved people, many fought back in whatever ways they could. Some fought back by working slowly or breaking tools.

Sometimes, enslaved people attacked their masters. Others destroyed the owners' property by starting fires in houses and barns.

Some enslaved people ran away. If caught, runaways were often killed. But thousands reached freedom in the North.

A few slaves organized armed rebellions against southern whites. The most famous

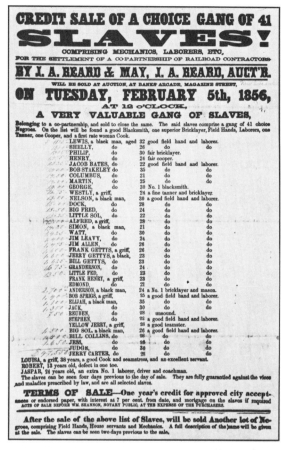

Library of Congress

slave rebellion was led by **Nat Turner**. In 1831, Turner led a small band of enslaved people against slaveholders in Virginia. Nearly 100 people were killed in the uprising. The Virginia militia finally caught the rebels and ended the rebellion.

Looking Back

1. How did owners control enslaved people?
2. How did enslaved people fight against their conditions?
3. Imagine you are a northern representative to Congress in 1850. Your state is against slavery. Tell Congress why you believe slavery is wrong.

The Slavery Debate

As you read in Chapter 10, most white southerners did not think slavery was wrong. They argued that slavery was necessary.

The South Defends Slavery

Many southern slaveholders pointed out that they depended on enslaved people to grow their crops. They argued that slaves were valuable property, like land and farm animals. They said that the Fifth Amendment to the Constitution protected a person's property. Asking a slaveholder to free his enslaved people was like asking him to give away his land.

Many southern whites were not slaveholders. But they still supported slavery. Slavery had been part of southern life for more than 200 years.

A Call for Equality

During the 1830s, some Americans began to call for an end to slavery and for *equality*, or equal treatment, for African Americans.

The attack on slavery was led by a group of reformers called *abolitionists*. Most abolitionists were northerners. Abolitionists believed that no one had the right to own another person. They worked to *abolish*, or end, slavery.

Abolitionists Speak Out

In the 1830s, abolitionists formed groups such as the American Anti-Slavery Society. They also published their own newspapers and printed articles that attacked slavery.

Abolitionist speakers traveled throughout the North, trying to convince Americans that slavery should be abolished.

The best speakers against slavery were people who had seen slavery up close. Some were former slaves, such as **Frederick Douglass** and **Sojourner Truth**. They helped people understand how it felt to be enslaved.

Other speakers were whites from the South, such as Sarah and Angelina Grimke, sisters from South Carolina. They had grown up hating the way enslaved people were treated on their plantation. Both had left the South and joined the abolitionists.

In 1852, **Harriet Beecher Stowe** wrote a book called *Uncle Tom's Cabin*. The book told stories she had heard from runaway slaves. It helped to turn the North against slavery.

In 1854, many Americans joined with abolitionists to form a new political party. They called it the **Republican Party**. Republican leaders promised to work in Congress to end slavery.

The Debate in Congress

The Missouri Compromise of 1820 banned slavery in the northern half of the Louisiana Territory. That included land that became Kansas Territory.

Then, in 1848, the United States won a war against Mexico. The United States won new territories in the Southwest as a result of the war. In Congress, the question most hotly debated was this: Should slavery be allowed in the new territories?

Looking Back

1. According to southerners, how did the Constitution protect the right to own slaves?
2. How did abolitionists attack slavery?
3. What did leaders of the new Republican Party promise to do?

FREE AND SLAVE STATES AND TERRITORY IN 1854

- ▦ Free states
- ▦ Free territories
- □ Popular sovereignty territories
- ▦ Slave states
- ▦ Slave territory

Slavery in the New Territories

In 1848, there were 15 free states and 15 slave states. Power between the North and the South was balanced in the Senate. Americans argued about the new territories that were won in the war with Mexico. Someday, those territories would become states.

Northerners wanted to forbid slavery in those new territories. Southerners wanted to allow slavery in them. They wanted to be able to outvote each other when the territories became states.

The South and North Compromise

Whenever northerners in Congress talked about forbidding slavery in the territories, southerners threatened to *secede*. They said they would leave the Union and form a new nation of southern states. Northerners did not want that.

In 1850, Congress agreed on a compromise. That agreement was called the **Compromise of 1850**. Northerners and southerners agreed that California would be a free state. Voters in the other territories would decide whether to allow slavery or not in their territories. The idea of letting the voters decide was called **popular sovereignty**.

Bloodshed in Kansas

In 1854, Congress argued about slavery in the Kansas Territory. The Missouri Compromise of 1820 had said that slavery would *not* be allowed in Kansas. But southerners believed that was unfair. Congress finally passed the **Kansas-Nebraska Act**. The Act repealed the Missouri Compromise. It divided the territory into the Kansas Territory and the Nebraska Territory. And it gave both territories popular sovereignty.

Settlers from the North and South raced into Kansas. Soon, bitter fighting broke out between those who were for slavery and those who were against it. Many settlers were killed.

The Dred Scott Decision

In 1857, the Supreme Court made an important *ruling*, or decision, about slavery. A slave named **Dred Scott** asked the Court to rule that he was a free man. His owner had taken him into a free state to live. Scott argued that his stay in a free state made him a free man.

The Supreme Court disagreed. The Court ruled that slaves were property. It said the Constitution protected the right of slaveowners to take their "property" anywhere. The ruling meant that owners could take slaves into any territory.

The Dred Scott decision was a victory for the South. But the decision did not end the slavery debate. Angry abolitionists and Republicans promised to continue to fight against slavery.

Looking Back

1. What did the Compromise of 1850 say about slavery in new territories?
2. What happened in Kansas when it was given popular sovereignty?
3. Why was the Dred Scott decision a victory for the South?

The Election of 1860

By 1860, the United States had two major political parties. One of them was the Democratic Party. The other party was the new Republican Party. It was only six years old. It had been started in 1854 by people who wanted to stop the spread of slavery.

The year of 1860 was a presidential election year. Slavery was the major issue in the election campaign.

The Democrats Split over Slavery

The Democratic Party was divided over the question of slavery in the territories. Northern Democrats wanted voters in each territory to decide for themselves about slavery. But southern Democrats were against popular sovereignty. They argued that slavery should be allowed everywhere.

The northern and southern Democrats held a convention to choose a candidate for President. The winner was a northerner, Stephen Douglas of Illinois. Angry southern Democrats walked out of the convention. They held their own convention and chose John C. Breckinridge of Kentucky to run for President.

The Republicans Campaign Against Slavery

The Republicans were sure they could win the election if they could win enough votes in the North.

At their convention, the Republicans wrote a *platform* that appealed to northern voters. (A platform is a list of the beliefs and ideas of a political party.) The Republican platform said that slavery should be kept out of the territories. The platform also promised to support tariffs and improvements in transportation.

The Republicans chose Abraham Lincoln to run for President. Lincoln was well known for his belief that slavery was wrong.

This 1886 drawing shows Abraham Lincoln.

Lincoln Wins

Some Americans were concerned about keeping the nation united. They formed a new party in 1860—the **Constitutional Union Party**. The party took no stand on slavery at all. In that way, it hoped to appeal to voters in both the North and the South. Party members chose John Bell of Tennessee to be their candidate.

The election results showed how divided the nation was. Lincoln won in every northern state except New Jersey. He did not win a single southern state. Southerners' votes were divided among Breckinridge, Douglas, and Bell. Because most of the North voted for Lincoln, he was elected President.

The Southern States Secede

Lincoln's victory worried southerners. Lincoln promised to leave slavery alone where it already existed, but southerners did not believe him. They talked about starting their own nation in the South.

In December 1860, South Carolina became the first state to secede from the Union. Mississippi, Florida, Alabama, Georgia, Louisiana, and Texas quickly followed. Those states joined together to form a new nation. That nation was called the **Confederate States of America**.

Looking Back
1. What argument split the Democratic Party in 1860?
2. What did the Republican platform say?
3. What does *secede* mean? Why did slave states secede from the Union?
4. What was the *Confederate States of America*?

Chapter 13

Review

Facts First

Write *North* next to the words that best describe the North. Write *South* next to the words that best describe the South.

1. was made up of the Northeast and the Midwest
2. included all the slave states
3. had most of the nation's factories
4. wanted high tariffs and better transportation
5. opposed high tariffs
6. feared a strong national government
7. was home for most African Americans
8. defended slavery
9. believed slavery was wrong
10. wanted to stop slavery from spreading into new territories
11. threatened to leave the Union if slavery was not protected
12. approved of the Dred Scott decision
13. voted for Breckinridge, Douglas, and Bell in 1860
14. voted for Lincoln in 1860
15. formed the Confederate States of America in 1861

Word Check

Write the meaning of each of these words. Then use each word in a sentence.

abolitionist	secede
economy	tariff

Skill Builder

Eleven southern states seceded to form the Confederate States of America at the beginning of the Civil War. Find out what those states were. Make a map of the 11 Confederate states. Use an encyclopedia or an almanac to help you.

Chapter 13 Notes

Read over the chapter. Find answers to these questions:

1. What were some differences between the North and the South in the mid-1800s?
2. Describe the life of an enslaved person on a southern plantation.
3. Who were the abolitionists? How did they fight slavery?
4. What did the Supreme Court say about slavery in the Dred Scott decision?
5. What did these groups want in the 1860 presidential election?
   a. northern Democrats
   b. southern Democrats
   c. Republicans
   d. Constitutional Union Party

Be a Historian

Enslaved people often made up songs. Many of those songs were religious. Such songs became known as *spirituals*. In spirituals, people often told of their wish to be free.

Listen to a record or tape of a spiritual. Or find the words of a spiritual in a book. Then tell what you think the words of the spiritual mean.

Bonus

1. Find out about one of these abolitionists. Then report what you learned.

John Brown	Sarah Grimke
Frederick Douglass	Harriet Beecher Stowe
William Lloyd Garrison	Sojourner Truth
Angelina Grimke	Harriet Tubman

2. Make a map of free states and territories in 1854.

Chapter 14 The American Civil War (1861-1865)

Library of Congress

A. Gardner made this photograph of Battery D, the 5th United States Artillery, after the battle at Fredericksburg, Virginia, in 1863.

By February 1861, seven states had seceded. The United States was divided into two parts: the Confederacy and the Union. Americans across the nation asked: Did states have the right to secede?

Southern leaders answered *yes.* They argued that the United States was a collection of separate states. The states had united with each other by free choice. Therefore, they had the right to secede if they chose and to set up a new nation.

Abraham Lincoln, the new President of the United States, disagreed. Lincoln said, ''A house divided against itself cannot stand.'' He meant that the United States could not survive if it was divided in two.

- Why did both the North and South enter the war confident of victory?
- How did African Americans fight for the Union?
- How did women help in the war?
- How did the Union win the war?

Key Words You will be using these words in this chapter. Look them up in the glossary at the back of Part 1.

assassination	**civil war**
blockade	**prejudice**

The War Begins

President Lincoln took office on March 4, 1861. In his inauguration speech, Lincoln urged the Confederate states to return to the Union. He said, ''We are not enemies, but friends.''

Lincoln hoped to bring the South back into the Union peacefully. But the differences between North and South were too great.

The Fall of Fort Sumter

When the southern states seceded, they tried to take over all the federal forts in their areas. However, some federal forts were able to hold out against the southerners. One of those was **Fort Sumter** in South Carolina. Fort Sumter was located on an island in Charleston harbor.

Confederate forces surrounded Fort Sumter. By April, the fort was running out of supplies. If Lincoln did not send help, the fort would have to surrender.

President Lincoln faced a difficult decision: If he sent troops to Fort Sumter, the South could say he had invaded their territory. That might start a *civil war.* But if Lincoln did nothing, and the fort surrendered, Americans might think that the federal government was not strong enough to hold the nation together. They might think that Lincoln was giving in to the South.

President Lincoln ordered the navy to take supplies to Fort Sumter. He told Confederate officials that the supplies were only food. But the southerners did not trust him. On April 12, 1861, Confederate forces fired heavy cannons on Fort Sumter. In the afternoon of the following day, the fort surrendered.

Union states

Confederate states

Border states

Fort Sumter

Four More Slave States Secede

The attack on Fort Sumter angered northerners. Lincoln called for 75,000 volunteers to join the Union army.

To southerners, Lincoln's call for troops was a declaration of war. Four more slave states—Virginia, North Carolina, Arkansas, and Tennessee—seceded from the Union. Now there were 11 Confederate states.

Four Border States Stay in the Union

Four slave states—Delaware, Maryland, Kentucky, and Missouri—stayed in the Union. Those states were called *border states* because they made up the border between the North and the South. (Part of Virginia also stayed in the Union and became West Virginia in 1863.)

Northerners Fight to Keep the Nation

Northerners believed they were fighting to hold the nation together. They thought the Union would quickly win the war because the Union was stronger than the Confederacy. The Union had more than twice as many people as the Confederacy, so it could raise a larger army. The Union also had a much larger navy.

The Union had most of the nation's factories and farms. Union factories could turn out military supplies for the army, such as rifles, ammunition, and uniforms. Union farms could grow enough food to keep the army well fed.

The Union had most of the nation's railroads. Railroads could carry food and supplies to the troops. They could also move troops quickly.

Southerners Fight for Their Way of Life

Southerners believed they were fighting for their independence and their way of life. Southerners compared their fight with America's War for Independence.

The Confederacy had fewer men and supplies than the Union. But many of the nation's best military leaders were southerners. At the start of the war, those leaders left the United States Army and joined the Confederate army.

The southern leaders planned to fight a *defensive war*. That meant that southern troops would stay in the South, fighting to defend their own land. Union troops would have to invade the South, fighting far from home and on land they did not know well.

Southerners believed that the Union would soon tire of the war. Then the Confederacy would be left alone. That would mean victory.

Looking Back

1. Why did Lincoln decide against sending troops to Fort Sumter?
2. How did the Civil War begin?
3. What reasons did each side give for fighting the war?
4. Why did the northerners think they were stronger?
5. Why did the southerners believe they would win?

The Union Plans a Quick Victory

Union leaders developed three main plans for defeating the Confederacy. One plan was to put an end to the Confederate government. To do that, Union forces would capture the Confederate capital—Richmond, Virginia.

The second plan was to cut off trade between the South and Europe. The South had few factories. So, the Confederacy had to buy military supplies from Europe. The Union planned to set up a **blockade** of southern ports. If the blockade worked, the South would not be able to ship cotton to Europe. And it would not be able to buy weapons and war supplies from Europe in return.

The third plan was to capture the Mississippi River and cut the Confederacy in half. Then Confederate states west of the Mississippi—Arkansas, Louisiana, and Texas—would not be able to send troops and supplies to the other Confederate states.

The First Battle of Bull Run

Union leaders moved quickly to carry out their first plan—the capture of Richmond. About 30,000 Union troops marched into Virginia from Washington, D.C. The troops did not have much training, but they were eager to invade the South.

The Union army met a smaller Confederate army at a stream called Bull Run. At first, Union troops seemed to be winning. But the Confederates, led by General **Thomas Jackson**, stood firm, "like a stonewall." They fought fiercely against the Union troops.

Later that day, more Confederate troops joined Jackson. Union troops panicked and ran back to Washington. Richmond was saved.

The Union Blocks the South

Union leaders carried out the second plan. They sent ships to block southern ports.

At first, the blockade was not very effective. The Union had only about 50 ships to patrol the long southern shoreline. Southern ships called *blockade-runners* sneaked past the blockade at night.

But by the end of 1861, Union shipyards had built more ships. Union forces also captured harbors along the coasts of North and South Carolina. Those harbors became the home ports for Union ships.

By 1865, the Union had over 600 ships blockading the South. Much-needed weapons and supplies never reached the Confederacy.

The Union Moves Toward the Mississippi

Early in 1862, Union leaders began to carry out the third plan—the capture of the Mississippi River. Union forces, led by **Ulysses Grant**, invaded Tennessee.

General Grant won two quick victories at Fort Henry and Fort Donelson. Then, on April 6, Confederate troops surprised Grant's army at Shiloh. For two days, Confederate and Union troops fought bitterly. Thousands of soldiers were wounded or killed. On the second day of the battle, Union troops arrived to save Grant from defeat.

After Shiloh, Union troops moved west and captured the city of Memphis on the Mississippi River. Meanwhile, the Union navy captured New Orleans. By the end of May, the Confederacy held only one city on the Mississippi—Vicksburg.

Looking Back

1. What three plans did the Union have for winning the war?
2. General Thomas Jackson became known as "Stonewall Jackson" at Bull Run. Why did that name fit him?
3. How did the Union's blockade make the war more difficult for the Confederacy?

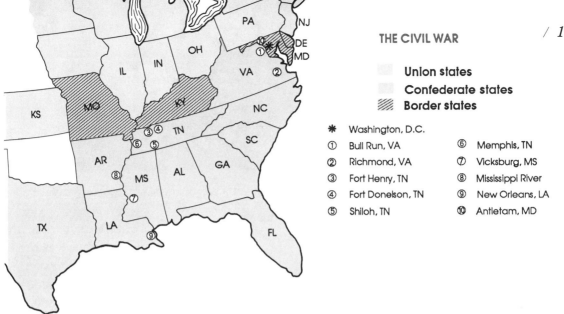

THE CIVIL WAR

Union states
Confederate states
Border states

✳ Washington, D.C.
① Bull Run, VA
② Richmond, VA
③ Fort Henry, TN
④ Fort Donelson, TN
⑤ Shiloh, TN
⑥ Memphis, TN
⑦ Vicksburg, MS
⑧ Mississippi River
⑨ New Orleans, LA
⑩ Antietam, MD

The War Becomes a Bitter Struggle

In March 1862, a Union army again invaded Virginia and marched toward the capital at Richmond. Confederate forces in Virginia were now led by General **Robert E. Lee.** Lee's troops defeated the Union army in a series of battles called the Seven Days' Battles.

In August, another Union army tried to capture Richmond. Lee's troops defeated that army in the Second Battle of Bull Run.

General Lee Invades the North

In September, General Lee invaded the North for the first time. Confederate leaders believed a victory in the North would damage Union morale. They believed a Confederate victory would force the Union to make peace.

Lee's army marched into Maryland. At Antietam, Lee's forces were attacked by a much larger Union army. In a few hours, 23,000 soldiers were killed or wounded. Lee was forced to retreat back into Virginia.

The Emancipation Proclamation

The battle at Antietam was a northern victory. But thousands of Union troops died at Antietam and in other battles. By 1862, many northerners wanted to stop fighting. They wondered if saving the Union was worth its cost in lives.

President Lincoln gave the North a reason to continue the fight. Lincoln announced on January 1, 1863, that all slaves in the states that were at war with the Union were now free. Lincoln's announcement was called the **Emancipation Proclamation**.

President Lincoln had no power over the states in the Confederacy. He could not really *emancipate*, or free, slaves there unless the North won the war. So, the Emancipation Proclamation gave the North a new reason to fight. The war became more than a fight to unite the nation. It was now a fight to end slavery.

Looking Back
1. Why did General Lee invade the North?
2. What was the Emancipation Proclamation?
3. How did the Emancipation Proclamation give the North a new reason to fight?

African Americans in the War

A black regiment fights in 1863 against Confederate troops.

In 1861, thousands of African Americans in the North volunteered for the Union army. But a federal law said that they could not become soldiers. So they became cooks, carpenters, and scouts instead.

Runaway slaves also tried to join the Union army. Some were allowed to work as laborers in army camps. But those from border states were returned to their owners.

African Americans Become Soldiers

Abolitionists protested the treatment of runaways and African American volunteers. In 1862, Union officers were ordered not to send runaways back into slavery. The government also repealed the law that stopped African Americans from becoming soldiers.

Frederick Douglass was a free man who had been born enslaved. He had become a well-known and respected author and lecturer. Douglass urged African Americans to become soldiers. Those "who would be free must strike the blow," he said.

By the end of the war, more than 185,000 African Americans had served in the Union army. Many of that number had fled the South and enlisted after the Emancipation Proclamation was issued. About 29,000 African Americans had served in the Union navy.

Army Life for African Americans

Army life helped many African Americans gain their self-respect. In army camps, African Americans were given a good meal, a bath, a haircut, and a uniform. For many, that uniform was the first suit of clothes they had ever owned. During training, former slaves learned to fight and handle weapons. Many also learned to read.

But there was another side to army life—*racial* **prejudice**. That was the belief that one race was not as good as another. Because of prejudice, African Americans were not treated the same as white soldiers at first. An African American soldier's *term of enlistment* was longer than a white's. (That was the length of time a soldier must serve.) African Americans were paid half as much as whites. They were put into all-black regiments under white officers. After training, African Americans were often handed shovels instead of guns. They could not become officers.

African Americans Demand Equal Treatment

Blacks wanted equal treatment. Many refused to accept any pay until they received equal pay. In 1864, Congress finally voted to pay black soldiers the same amount as whites.

The nation honored many African American soldiers for their courage. Twenty-one received the Medal of Honor, the highest award given to Union soldiers.

Looking Back

1. How were African Americans treated unfairly in the army?
2. What actions did Congress take to give African Americans more equal rights?
3. What award did the Union give to 21 black soldiers? What was the award for?

Clara Barton risked her life to nurse wounded men on the battlefields of the Civil War. This U.S. postage stamp honors her.

Left: Belle Boyd, a Confederate spy, was an expert in codes. Right: Harriet Tubman was a spy who helped many slaves escape to join the Union army.

Women in the War

Women in both the North and South helped throughout the war. When men marched off to fight, women stayed home to plant and harvest the crops. They also sewed uniforms and blankets. In the North, women took men's places in factories. In the North and South, women's aid societies collected money, bandages, and food for the soldiers.

Help on the Battlefields and Behind the Lines

Many women also served as nurses during the war. Some nurses, such as **Clara Barton**, risked their lives to treat soldiers on the battlefields.

African American women also served as nurses for the Union army. Some, such as **Susie King Taylor**, also taught African American soldiers to read and write.

In the South, black women helped the Union in other ways. They gave directions to lost Union soldiers. They helped Union troops find food and horses. They hid Union soldiers who had escaped from Confederate prisons.

Soldiers and Spies

Women also served their armies as soldiers and spies. Their work helped both sides in the war.

Harriet Tubman spied for the Union. Her best information came from enslaved people who had listened to their owners talk. Tubman helped many slaves escape and join the Union army. She also led black regiments on raids into the South. Her soldiers called her General Tubman.

Belle Boyd was a Confederate spy. At the age of 17, she was an expert in the use of secret codes. In the North, she found out about Union troop movements, then coded that information and sent it to the Confederate army. She was captured three times but always released.

Sarah Edmonds joined the Union army as "Frank Thompson" and fought in several battles. During that time, while pretending to be a man, she offered to "pretend" to be a woman in order to spy. Dressed as a woman, Sarah Edmonds traveled behind Confederate lines. There she gathered useful information to take back to the North.

Looking Back
1. How did women at home help during the war?
2. How were women involved in the fighting of the war?
3. In what ways do women serve their country today?

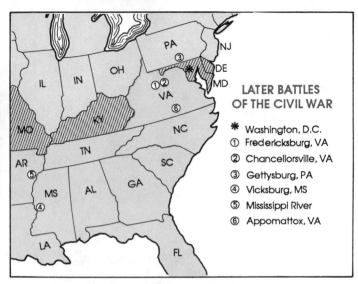

This U.S. postage stamp honors President Abraham Lincoln.

LATER BATTLES OF THE CIVIL WAR

* Washington, D.C.
① Fredericksburg, VA
② Chancellorsville, VA
③ Gettysburg, PA
④ Vicksburg, MS
⑤ Mississippi River
⑥ Appomattox, VA

The Union Gains Control

By 1863, the Union blockade was working well. The Confederacy was running short of military supplies. But spirits in the South remained high. The Confederacy still expected to win the war.

Gettysburg: the Turning Point

By May 1863, Confederate forces under Robert E. Lee had stopped two more invasions of Virginia—at Fredericksburg and Chancellorsville. Lee decided to again invade the North.

General Lee's army crossed Maryland and moved into Pennsylvania. Confederate and Union forces met near the town of **Gettysburg**. The two armies battled for three days.

Then, on July 3, Confederate troops attacked a key Union position on a hill called Cemetery Ridge. Confederate troops fought bravely. But Union bullets drove them back. Lee's forces suffered terrible losses. Lee was forced to withdraw from Gettysburg and return to Virginia. The North had won a great victory.

Gettysburg was a turning point in the war. More than 20,000 Confederate soldiers were killed or wounded. Never again would Lee's army be strong enough to invade the North.

The Gettysburg Address

Seven thousand Union troops died at Gettysburg. Four months after the battle, Lincoln traveled to Gettysburg to honor the dead. He gave a speech called the **Gettysburg Address**.

In that speech, Lincoln talked about the war's meaning. The fallen soldiers, he said, had not "died in vain." They had fought and died to give the nation "a new birth of freedom."

The Union Controls the Mississippi River

In July 1863, the Union won another great victory. That victory was in the West. For more than six weeks, Union forces under General Grant had been attacking Vicksburg, Mississippi. On July 4, Vicksburg surrendered.

The fall of Vicksburg meant that the Union now controlled the Mississippi River. The Confederacy was cut in two.

Looking Back

1. Why was Gettysburg a turning point in in the war?
2. Why was Vicksburg an important Union victory?
3. What do you think President Lincoln meant when he said that soldiers had died to give the nation "a new birth of freedom"?

General Grant is shown with some of the officers who fought with him. General Grant stands in the center of the photograph, with his hands in his pockets. At far right sits Colonel Ely S. Parker, a Native American and chief of the tribes known as the *Six Nations*

Grant Takes Command

President Lincoln was pleased with General Grant's victories. In March 1864, he made Grant the commander of all Union forces. Grant came up with a plan for the final defeat of the Confederacy.

Grant's plan was this: He would take charge of the Union army in the East. That army would battle Lee's forces in Virginia.

Meanwhile, the Union army in the West would move east through Georgia. After defeating southern troops in Georgia, the army would move north through South Carolina and North Carolina. In Virginia, the two Union armies would join together. They would then crush General Lee's army and capture Richmond.

Marching Through Georgia

General **William Tecumseh Sherman** led the Union army that marched into Georgia. Grant ordered General Sherman to destroy anything that might be useful to Confederate forces still fighting the war.

During their march through Georgia, Sherman's troops destroyed crops and farm animals and burned barns and houses. They tore up railroad tracks, heated them redhot, and twisted them into ''Sherman's hairpins.'' They wrecked bridges. They also burned towns and cities, including Atlanta, Georgia.

In December 1864, Sherman's army reached Savannah, Georgia, on the Atlantic Ocean. Behind the army lay a path of destruction 60 miles wide and 300 miles long. For years after the war, southerners would bitterly remember Sherman's ''march to the sea.''

Looking Back
1. How did Ulysses Grant become the commander of all Union forces in 1864?
2. What was the Union plan for the final defeat of the Confederacy?
3. Why were southerners bitter about General Sherman's march to the sea?

The New-York Times.

VOL. XIV.....NO. 4230.

NEW-YORK, SATURDAY, APRIL 15, 1865.

PRICE FOUR CENTS

AWFUL EVENT.

President Lincoln Shot by an Assassin.

The Deed Done at Ford's Theatre Last Night.

THE ACT OF A DESPERATE REBEL

The President Still Alive at ...

EUROPEAN NEWS.

TWO DAYS LATER BY THE EUROPA.

The Insult to Our Cruisers by Portugal.

The American Minister at Lisbon Demands Satisfaction.

Dismissal of the Commander of Fort Belan Requested.

Further Advance in Five-T'wenties.

FINANCIAL AND COMMERCIAL.

The War Ends

By early 1865, the Confederacy was near defeat. Sherman had conquered Georgia and was marching north toward Virginia. In Virginia, Grant's army had pushed to within a few miles of Richmond.

Surrender at Appomattox

During 1864 and early 1865, Grant and Lee had fought across Virginia. Their armies had suffered heavy losses. Grant had lost nearly 60,000 troops. Lee had lost nearly 30,000. But Grant could replace his fallen soldiers with more troops from the North. The South had no more men to call into service.

By spring, Lee's army was also out of supplies. Many soldiers were hungry and barefooted. The army could no longer protect the capital at Richmond. On April 3, 1865, Union troops entered the city. On April 9, Lee surrendered to Grant at **Appomattox**, Virginia. The war was over.

Grant's terms of surrender were generous: Confederate soldiers gave up their weapons but were not held as prisoners. They were free to return home in peace. They could keep their horses and mules to work their farms.

Across the North, news of Lee's surrender brought wild celebration. In the South, there was deep sadness.

The Death of Lincoln

A few days after the surrender at Appomattox, President Lincoln went to a play at Ford's Theater in Washington. An actor named **John Wilkes Booth** silently entered the President's box, pointed a gun at the President, and shot him. By morning, the President was dead.

The **assassination**, or murder, of Lincoln stunned the North. Lincoln had led the nation through its darkest time. He had saved the Union and ended slavery. His death was a terrible loss.

Some southerners cheered when they heard of Lincoln's death. But the Confederate president, **Jefferson Davis**, saw nothing to cheer about. Before his death, Lincoln had spoken of a "just [fair] and lasting peace." He asked all Americans to join together and "bind up the nation's wounds." Davis and other southerners feared that with Lincoln gone, the wounds of war would be slow to heal.

Looking Back
1. Why did General Lee surrender?
2. What were the terms of surrender?
3. What did Lincoln hope would happen in the nation after the war?
4. Why could Lincoln's death be called a loss for both the North and the South?

Chapter 14

Review

Facts First

Write *Union* next to each statement that describes the Union. Write *Confederacy* next to each statement that describes the Confederacy.

1. fired on Fort Sumter
2. fought to keep the nation united and to free the slaves
3. fought to be independent and to keep its way of life
4. strengths included more people, farms, factories, and railroads
5. fought mainly a defensive war
6. had its capital at Richmond, Virginia
7. needed military supplies from Europe
8. set up a blockade
9. used blockade-runners
10. let African Americans become soldiers and sailors
11. won control of the Mississippi River
12. had a general named Ulysses Grant
13. had a general named Robert E. Lee
14. won battles at Bull Run, Chancellorsville, and Fredericksburg
15. won battles at Antietam, Gettysburg, and Vicksburg

Word Check

Write the meanings of these words. Then use them in sentences.

> **assassination**   **civil war**
> **blockade**   **prejudice**

Skill Builder

Find out about one of these important people from America's past. Then report what you learned.

Clara Barton   George McClellan
Jefferson Davis   George Pickett
Robert E. Lee   James "Jeb" Stuart
Abraham Lincoln   Susie King Taylor

Chapter 14 Notes

Read over the chapter. Find answers to these questions:

1. Why did the Union and the Confederacy each expect to win the war?
2. What was the Emancipation Proclamation, and why was it made?
3. What was life in the army like for African American volunteers?
4. What were the terms of surrender given to General Lee at Appomattox?
5. Why did many people in the North and South consider Lincoln's death a loss?

Be a Historian

During the Civil War, African American soldiers faced racial prejudice. Find out how the armed forces deal with racial prejudice these days. Interview someone who is in the military. (One place to find such a person is the armed forces' recruiting office in your town.) Ask that person these questions:

1. Do people of all races live and train together?
2. Can people of all races become officers?
3. What is the military doing to fight racial prejudice?
4. If someone in the military is a victim of racial prejudice, what can that person do?

Bonus

Throughout America's history, there have been groups of Americans who have been against war. Those people are called *pacifists*. They believe in peaceful ways to solve differences. Find out more about pacifists and *pacifism*.

Chapter 15 Reconstruction (1865-1877)

Library of Congress

These stereoscope photographs show the ruins of Richmond, Virginia, after the Civil War.

The Civil War answered the question of secession. The South would still be part of the United States. It was time now to *reconstruct*, or rebuild, the South. But the *reconstruction* of the South raised new questions.

How should the southern states be treated? Should they be punished for starting the war? Or should they be forgiven and welcomed back into the Union?

And what about the four million freed slaves in the South? How could they be helped to build new lives? Should they have the same rights as white citizens?

From 1865 to 1877—the years of reconstruction—Americans struggled to answer those questions.

- How did the war damage the South?
- What were the problems of reconstruction?
- How did freedom change the lives of former slaves?
- Why did many whites in the South oppose reconstruction?

Key Words   You will be using these words in this chapter. Look them up in the glossary at the back of Part 1.

civil rights	**impeach**
corrupt	**terrorism**

The South in Ruins

The South paid a terrible price for the war. Over 250,000 Confederate soldiers died in the war—a third of southern white males. Soldiers who survived were often sick or wounded. Many were so thin that their families did not recognize them.

Southern cities were in ruins, destroyed in the fighting. An eyewitness described Columbia, South Carolina, as ''a wilderness of ruins.'' The center of the city was ''a mass of blackened chimneys and crumbling walls.'' Another eyewitness, in Georgia, described the ''broad black streak of ruin'' left by Sherman's troops. Piles of rubble were all that was left of houses. Railroads, farms, stores, factories—all lay in ruins.

Economy and Government Collapse

The southern economy was also in ruins. It had been based on farming and slave labor. But slavery was illegal now, and Confederate money worthless. Many farms in the South had been burned. Farmers had no money to rebuild their homes or even to buy the seeds needed to start a new crop.

Throughout the South, state governments collapsed. Law and order broke down in many places in the South. Groups of outlaws roamed the countryside, robbing and killing.

Looking Back
1. What had the southern economy been based on before the war?
2. How were southern cities and farms affected by the war?
3. What happened to state governments and law and order in many places in the South after the war?

Life in the South—After the War

The years that followed the war were hard for both white and black people in the South. Rebuilding their lives proved to be a difficult job.

African American Southerners

After the war, slaveholders often turned their slaves free with nowhere to go. So, although African Americans were free, many were hungry and homeless.

Many blacks roamed southern roads. Some were looking for loved ones who had been sent to other plantations. But most were looking for work, food, and a place to live.

The Freedmen's Bureau

In March 1865, Congress set up the **Freedmen's Bureau** to help freed slaves. The Freedmen's Bureau gave food and clothing to both blacks and whites. It built hospitals throughout the South. It also set up schools for African Americans and helped them find work at fair pay.

New Beginnings

Once the shock of defeat passed, southerners began to rebuild. New buildings went up in cities. Railroad lines were repaired. Factories began to run again. They produced textiles, furniture, and other goods. Some southerners found work in those factories.

But farming was still the most important *occupation* (work) in the South. Landowners began to plow and plant their lands. They wanted to ship cotton, sugar, and tobacco out of southern ports again.

Farmers Turn to Sharecropping

Before the war, enslaved people had worked on the farms and plantations. They had planted and harvested the crops that landowners sold. After the slaves were freed, landowners had to pay the people who worked for them.

Some landowners had money to pay workers. But most did not. So, many turned to a system of farming called **sharecropping**. In sharecropping, a landowner rents land to a farmer. The landowner then gets a share of the farmer's crop.

Sharecroppers Face Growing Debts

Here is how sharecropping worked: The landowner rented a piece of land to a *sharecropper*—the person who wanted to farm. The sharecropper grew and harvested a cash crop, such as tobacco, cotton, or peanuts. The crop was then divided into two *shares*. One share, usually the larger, went to the landowner as rent. The sharecropper kept the rest of the crop.

Many blacks and poor whites became sharecroppers. They hoped to make enough money to buy their own land. Instead, they usually went into debt.

Sharecroppers were not paid any wages. To feed and clothe their families until harvest time, they borrowed money. In good years, sharecroppers made enough money to pay their debts. But most years were not good, and they remained poor.

Looking Back

1. What problems did freed African Americans face right after the war?
2. How did the Freedmen's Bureau help southerners?
3. What was sharecropping?
4. Why did sharecroppers go into debt?

The Struggle over Reconstruction

Tickets were sold for the impeachment trial of President Johnson.

Toward the end of the Civil War, President Lincoln had drawn up a plan for reconstruction. He wanted to bring the southern states quickly back into the Union.

Lincoln's plan was this: Former citizens of the Confederacy had to swear loyalty to the United States. When ten percent of a state's voters had sworn their loyalty, the state could form a new government. The state could then rejoin the Union.

Andrew Johnson Takes Over

After Lincoln died on April 15, 1865, the Vice-President, **Andrew Johnson**, became President. Johnson was a southerner who had remained loyal to the Union. Like most southerners, he feared a strong federal government. As President, he wanted to limit the government's powers to those listed in the Constitution.

In May 1865, Johnson announced his own reconstruction plan. Johnson's plan was much like Lincoln's, but it also required southern states to approve the **Thirteenth Amendment** to the Constitution. That amendment abolished slavery throughout the United States.

Eight southern states then organized new state governments and attempted to meet Johnson's requirements. At the end of 1865, the Thirteenth Amendment was ratified, and the President was satisfied that reconstruction was over.

Congress Opposes the President

Republicans in Congress disagreed with President Johnson. They were angry because neither Lincoln nor Johnson had *consulted*, or asked, Congress about reconstruction. They said that Congress, not the President, should control reconstruction.

Republicans said that President Johnson was too easy on the South. Johnson had *pardoned* (forgiven) many Confederate *rebels*—southerners who had fought or worked for the Confederacy. Those people were now leading their new state governments.

The South Passes Black Codes

Republicans also disliked Johnson's plan for reconstruction. They said it did not go far enough to protect the rights of southern African Americans. Some new southern state governments that had been organized under Johnson's plan were passing laws called **black codes**.

Black codes said that African Americans could not vote, hold office, or serve on juries. They could not meet together after dark or own guns. They could not become doctors or lawyers. And African Americans without jobs could be arrested or hired out to planters. Republicans were furious about the black codes. They said the codes set up a new kind of slavery.

Southern Congressmen Are Turned Away

Under Johnson's plan, southern voters could once more elect members to Congress. In December 1865, the newly elected members arrived in Washington to take their seats. Some of them were former Confederate rebels. Republicans in Congress voted not to let any of the southerners sit in Congress.

Looking Back

1. What was the Thirteenth Amendment?
2. Why did Congress oppose President Johnson's plan for reconstruction?
3. What were the black codes?

This engraving from *Harper's Weekly* shows President Johnson's impeachment trial.

Congress Acts Against the President

Congress passed two bills. The first gave the Freedmen's Bureau more power. The second attacked the black codes. It said African Americans had the same *civil rights* as whites.

Johnson vetoed both bills. He said they went beyond the powers given to the government by the Constitution. Congress overrode his veto. Then it rewrote the civil rights bill as the **Fourteenth Amendment** to the Constitution.

The Fourteenth Amendment

The amendment said that anyone born in the United States was a citizen of the nation. That meant African Americans were citizens with full civil rights.

The amendment also said that former Confederate soldiers and officials could not hold any state or national office.

Congress Takes Over Reconstruction

In 1867, Congress passed a bill for its own plan for reconstruction. President Johnson vetoed the bill. Again, Congress voted to override the President's veto.

The new plan overturned Johnson's plan for reconstruction. It did not recognize Confederate states as being back in the Union. Southern state governments that had been set up under Johnson's plan were abolished.

Congress then set up *military rule* in the South. The South was divided into five military districts. A general ruled each district. Troops were sent to keep order.

Congress Sets Three Main Terms

To end military rule and rejoin the Union, southern states had to meet these three terms set by Congress:

First, each state had to write a new constitution, which guaranteed African American males the right to vote and hold office. Only African American and white males who had not supported the Confederacy could vote for the delegates to write that constitution.

Second, voters had to elect leaders who were not former Confederates.

And, third, each state legislature had to approve the Fourteenth Amendment.

By 1868, the Fourteenth Amendment had been ratified. And by 1871, all the southern states had rejoined the Union.

Congress Impeaches Andrew Johnson

President Johnson continued to fight with Congress about its reconstruction plan. In 1868, Congress tried to remove Johnson from office.

The Constitution says that Congress can remove a President. The House of Representatives must first *impeach* him. That means it must accuse him of doing something illegal. The President then goes on trial in the Senate. If two-thirds of the senators find the President guilty of ''high crimes,'' the Senate can then vote to remove him from office.

Johnson was impeached, but Congress could not prove that he had broken any law. The Senate voted that the President was not guilty—but by only one vote.

Looking Back

1. What did the Fourteenth Amendment say?
2. Under the reconstruction plan made by Congress, what three things did a state have to do to rejoin the Union?
3. Why was President Johnson impeached? Was he removed from office?

These students are in a school in Charleston, South Carolina. This sketch was done in the 1870s.

The New African American Citizens

The Fourteenth Amendment was ratified in 1868. The Constitution now made it clear that enslaved African Americans were now free citizens of the United States. They began to learn how to live as free people.

Education

During slavery, it was illegal to give enslaved people an education. When slaves were freed, they were eager to learn how to read and write.

The Freedmen's Bureau helped build 4000 schools for African Americans. Those were the first free schools in the South. African Americans crowded into the schools. Often, children, parents, and grandparents learned to read and write together.

The Freedmen's Bureau also helped set up the first colleges for African Americans, who raised money to support those colleges. African Americans worked hard to save money to send their children to college. For many, the right to go to school became the key to a better life.

New Constitutions

An important new right for African Americans was the right to vote. African Americans first voted in the South in 1867, when they elected delegates to the state constitutional conventions. Many of the delegates elected were African American. They played an important role in writing the new constitutions.

The new constitutions brought needed changes to the South. They gave the vote to all men, both black and white. They improved the treatment of poor people and lawbreakers. In the past, poor people who could not pay their debts were put in jail. Lawbreakers were whipped or branded with hot irons. The constitutions put a stop to those kinds of treatment.

Before the Civil War, only the children of wealthy planters received an education. The new constitutions set up the first *public school systems* in the South. (In a public school system, students attend school free. State tax money pays for the schools.) For the first time, all children—both black and white—could go to school.

These African Americans were elected to Congress during reconstruction. *Right*: This engraving is part of a Currier & Ives print. *Above*: Senator Blanche K. Bruce.

African American Politicians

After constitutions were approved, state elections were held. For the first time, African Americans were elected to public office. They won many local offices, such as mayor and justice of the peace.

African Americans also won state offices. In three states, they were elected lieutenant governor. Every state legislature in the South had African American members. These lawmakers worked hard to build the new public school systems. They tried to improve life for the poor. In Georgia, African American lawmakers tried to pass bills giving women the right to vote.

African Americans were also elected to Congress. Mississippi voters elected the nation's first black senators. They were **Hiram R. Revels** and **Blanche K. Bruce**. Other states elected African Americans to serve in the House of Representatives.

Despite these gains for African Americans, all the state governors were white. And in nearly every state legislature, a majority of the members were white.

Making a Living

Most African Americans remained poor in the years following the war. Formerly enslaved, they had no land, tools, or money. In the first years of freedom, many died of starvation or disease.

African Americans looked for work wherever they could. Most remained in farming areas. They worked as field hands or sharecroppers. A few were able to buy their own land.

Many African American women found jobs as cooks and household servants. Some African American men looked for work in the factories and shipyards of the cities, but white workers had most of those jobs. If a black man found work in a factory or shipyard, he was usually paid less than a white man doing the same job.

Reconstruction was a time of struggle for most African Americans. But it was also a time of hope, opportunity, and freedom.

Looking Back

1. Why were African Americans eager to go to school?
2. How did the new state constitutions help both black and white men?
3. How did African Americans take part in their state governments? in the nation's government?
4. Why do you think blacks were paid less than whites for doing the same work?

The South During Reconstruction

The reconstruction of the South lasted from 1865 to 1877. To whites who had supported the Confederacy, it was a terrible time. When the war ended, they thought that southern politics would be the way it had been before the war: Whites would still control African Americans. Planters would still be the leaders of their state governments. And government leaders would still be Democrats.

Politics Under Reconstruction

Life under reconstruction turned out to be very different. Former Confederates could not vote or hold office. And the new South came under the control of new groups. Those groups elected Republican leaders throughout the South.

Some of those leaders were African Americans. But most were whites who had never held office before. Many were northerners who came South after the war. They carried a *carpetbag*, which was a small suitcase, so they were called **carpetbaggers**. Many southerners believed the carpetbaggers were ***corrupt*** northerners who had come South to make a fortune.

Other new White leaders were southerners who had stayed loyal to the Union. Former Confederates hated them. They called them **scalawags**, or rascals.

Complaints Against the Governments

Many southerners, especially former Confederates, opposed the reconstruction governments and their leaders. They complained that the governments set taxes too high. They charged that the new leaders knew nothing about running the government. They also claimed that there was *corruption*, or dishonesty, in the governments. They said leaders took bribes and stole tax money.

There was some truth to those charges. Taxes were high: They were needed to rebuild the schools, roads, and hospitals of the South. And some government officials were corrupt.

During 1868 and 1869, many white southerners began working to get rid of Republican officeholders. They wanted to put Democrats back into their governments. One way to do that was to keep African Americans from voting.

Terrorism Against African Americans

Without black votes, Republicans could not win elections in the South. To keep blacks from voting, some whites used ***terrorism***. Terrorism is the use of violence and fear to control people.

Secret societies, such as the **Ku Klux Klan**, were formed to frighten African Americans. The Klan did its work at night. Mobs of white men put on white robes and hoods that covered their faces and hid their identities. They broke up Republican meetings. They woke up blacks and white Republicans and told them not to vote. They beat, whipped, and sometimes murdered those who tried to vote.

The Fifteenth Amendment

In 1869, Congress tried to protect voters. It proposed an amendment that said that a person could not be kept from voting because of race or color. In 1870, that amendment was approved by the states. It became the **Fifteenth Amendment** to the Constitution.

In 1870 and 1871, Congress passed the **Force Act** and the **Ku Klux Klan Act**. Those laws said that anyone who tried to keep a person from voting could be fined or arrested. Federal troops in the South arrested hundreds of whites under those laws. But violence against African Americans continued.

Courtesy The Historic New Orleans Collection, Museum/Research Center,
Acc. No. 1974.25.9.213

Library of Congress

Ku Klux Klansmen in hoods, hats, and masks threaten to murder their victim. This engraving is of an actual event that happened in 1871.

Federal troops march out of Orleans Hotel, New Orleans, Louisiana, in April 1877.

Reconstruction Ends

In 1876, federal troops remained in the three southern states still under Republican governments. Many northerners believed it was time to withdraw those troops and end reconstruction. They believed that reconstruction had gone on long enough.

Northerners had also heard stories about corruption in the reconstruction governments. Ulysses Grant had been President since 1868. During his terms, corruption was widespread in the federal government. Americans wanted an end to all corruption in government.

In March 1877, **Rutherford Hayes** was inaugurated as the new President. In April, President Hayes withdrew the last federal troops from the South. Twelve years of reconstruction came to an end.

Within a year, white Democratic governments were in place in every southern state. Under those governments, African Americans would lose many of the rights and opportunities they had gained during reconstruction.

The Democrats Take Control

Violence was not the only way African Americans were kept from voting. Most worked for whites. They were told they would lose their jobs if they voted, and, out of fear, many stopped voting. Voting places were also hidden from African Americans.

White Democrats took control of one state after another. They stuffed *ballot boxes* with votes that were illegal. (Ballot boxes are the boxes voters put their votes in.) They destroyed the votes of African Americans who continued to vote. As one black man from Georgia said, "A hole gets in the bottom of the [ballot] boxes some way and lets out our votes."

Republicans began to lose elections throughout the South. In 1870, Democrats took control in Virginia, North Carolina, and Georgia. By 1876, only three southern states still had Republican governments: Louisiana, South Carolina, and Florida.

Looking Back

1. What people were called carpetbaggers and scalawags by white southerners? Why?
2. How did some southern whites try to keep blacks from voting?
3. What was the Fifteenth Amendment?
4. How did white Democrats regain control of southern governments?
5. Why did northerners begin to feel that reconstruction should end?
6. The Fifteenth Amendment protects the right of people to vote, regardless of race or color. Why do you think the right to vote is important?

Chapter 15

Review

Facts First

Use the words below to complete each sentence.

Abraham Lincoln	**Freedmen's Bureau**
African American	**Ku Klux Klan**
males	**reconstruction**
carpetbaggers	**Republican**
Congress	**Rutherford Hayes**
Democratic	

1. The plan for bringing the South back into the Union was called _____.
2. _____ came up with the first reconstruction plan.
3. For three years, Andrew Johnson and _____ fought for control of reconstruction.
4. New state constitutions in the South gave _____ the right to vote.
5. The _____ set up African American schools in the South.
6. Northerners who became leaders in southern governments were called _____.
7. Most leaders in reconstruction governments belonged to the _____ Party.
8. Groups such as the _____ threatened African American voters.
9. _____ withdrew federal troops from the South, ending reconstruction.
10. By 1877, the _____ Party controlled every state government in the South.

Word Check

Write the meanings of these words. Then use them in sentences.

civil rights	**impeach**
corrupt	**terrorism**

Skill Builder

Find out in what years these events happened. Then write them in order.

- The last federal troops leave the South.
- Congress takes over reconstruction.
- Andrew Johnson becomes President after Abraham Lincoln is assassinated.
- African Americans become officeholders in the South.
- Democrats control all the governments in the South.

Chapter 15 Notes

Read over the chapter. Find answers to these questions:

1. What problems did white southern farmers face after the war ended?
2. What problems did southern blacks face?
3. Describe:
   a. President Johnson's reconstruction plan.
   b. the three-part plan of Congress for reconstruction.
4. What were white southerners' complaints about the new leaders and new governments of reconstruction?
5. How were the following meant to help African Americans?
   a. Freedmen's Bureau
   b. Thirteenth Amendment
   c. Fourteenth Amendment
   d. Fifteenth Amendment
   e. Force Act and Ku Klux Klan Act

Be a Historian

Thirty colleges for African Americans were started during reconstruction. Four are:

- Hampton University
- Morehouse College
- Howard University
- Tuskegee University

Find out about one of those colleges. Write a report about it.

Unit 5  Review

What Do You Know?

Complete each sentence by choosing the correct ending.

1. In the 1850s, sectionalism
   a. brought the nation together.
   b. did not exist in America.
   c. threatened to divide the nation.
2. The issue that most divided the North and South was
   a. women's rights.
   b. slavery.
   c. treatment of the Indians.
3. The election of Lincoln in 1860
   a. pleased southerners.
   b. led to secession in the South.
   c. united the North and the South.
4. Lincoln's Emancipation Proclamation
   a. ended the Civil War.
   b. was a plan for reconstruction.
   c. was about freedom for enslaved people.
5. The Civil War ended when
   a. Lincoln was killed.
   b. Lee surrendered at Appomattox.
   c. Lee won at Gettysburg.
6. Reconstruction was the plan
   a. to rebuild Richmond, Virginia.
   b. to bring the South back into the Union.
   c. to win the war by blockading the South.
7. When reconstruction ended,
   a. prejudice was gone from the South.
   b. Democrats won control of the South.
   c. many African Americans still held offices in the South.

What Do You Think?

Prejudice is still a problem in America today.

1. What groups suffer from prejudice?
2. What do you think causes prejudice?
3. What can you do to help end prejudice?

Skill Builder

Find out in what years these events happened. Then write them in order.

- The Republican Party is organized.
- The Fourteenth Amendment, making African Americans U.S. citizens, is ratified.
- The Thirteenth Amendment, abolishing slavery, is ratified.
- Lincoln issues the Emancipation Proclamation.
- The Fifteenth Amendment, protecting voting rights, is ratified.

Unit 5 Notes

Look over the unit to find answers to these questions:

1. How were the North and the South different from each other before the Civil War?
2. Why did southern states secede after Lincoln won the election in 1860?
3. What did Lincoln say in the Emancipation Proclamation?
4. What terms of surrender did General Grant present to General Lee?
5. According to Congress, what did southern states have to do to rejoin the Union?
6. How did white southerners regain control of the South?

Word Builder

Write a story about the South during reconstruction. Use all the key words listed below.

Key Words

civil rights	corrupt	prejudice
civil war	economy	terrorism

Glossary Part 1

ab o li tion ist a person who wants to abolish, or end, slavery

a dapt to change how one lives in order to survive in a new situation *The people adapted to the new land that they moved to.*

al li ance an agreement between countries to help one another

a mend ment an addition to the Constitution

an nex to join or add new land to a state or country

ar che ol o gist a scientist who studies how people lived in ancient times

ar ti fact an object that a person made in ancient times *Scientists find out about the first Americans by studying their artifacts.*

as sas si na tion the murder of a leader or other important person

block ade an action by military forces to block, or stop, people and supplies from going into an area *The navy blockade kept ships from entering the harbor.*

bor der land or water right next to the dividing line between two states or nations

bound ary the dividing line that separates a territory, state, or nation from other territories, states, or nations

boy cott to refuse to buy or use certain products *The colonists boycotted British goods.*

cab i net the group of government department heads who advise the President

cen sus a count done by the government of all the people in the country *A census of Americans is taken every ten years.*

civ il rights rights, given by law, that belong to the people of a nation *Voting is one of our civil rights.*

civ il war a war fought between groups of people who live in the same country

col o ny a settlement set up by people far from their home country, but ruled by the home country

com mu ni cate to share or exchange news and other information

com pro mise an agreement in which everyone gives up something to end a disagreement

cor rupt dishonest; willing to do wrong and illegal acts *Corrupt officials took bribes and stole tax money.*

del e gate a person chosen by others to speak for and represent them at a meeting

de moc ra cy a government run by the people *In a democracy, people elect their leaders.*

de scen dant a person born in a certain family group; a child, grandchild, great-grandchild, etc. *She is a descendant of the first people to come to America.*

dis ease sickness *Many pioneers died of diseases such as smallpox.*

e con o my the businesses, industries, and trade of a nation *When the economy is good, people in the nation have money to spend.*

e lec tion choosing leaders or laws by voting for them

em pire many nations, territories, and peoples controlled by one government *The British empire governed nations in Africa, Asia, and North America.*

ex pan sion getting larger by gaining more territory *America's expansion resulted in several new states for the Union.*

ex pe di tion a group of people making a journey for certain reasons, such as exploring new territory

fac to ry a place where many workers make the goods that a business sells *He works in a **factory** that makes clothes.*

fed er al of the nation; national *The **federal** government makes laws for the nation.*

found ed set up or started *The Pilgrims **founded** a colony in 1620.*

fron tier the farthest edge of settled territory; land unsettled by pioneers *The land west of the Appalachian Mountains was the **frontier** of the new United States.*

im mi grant a person who moves to another country or territory to live there

im peach to legally accuse a government official of doing something against the law or the Constitution

in de pen dence freedom; a people's right to rule themselves

in vent to create or think up a new thing or way of doing something *He **invented** a machine that made cloth.*

leg is la ture a group of people who have the power to make laws *Congress is our nation's **legislature**.*

lim it to keep from going too far; restrict *The Constitution **limits** the powers of the federal government.*

mi li tia an army made up of citizens who are not full-time soldiers *The National Guard is a **militia**.*

na tion al having to do with the nation as a whole *The **national** government governs the whole country.*

pi o neer one of the first people to go into and live in a new land

po lit i cal par ty a group of people who have the same ideas about government

prej u dice disliking a person or group for no good reason

pro duce to make or manufacture goods to be sold by a business

rat i fy to officially agree to or approve *Nine states had to **ratify** the Constitution before it became law.*

re bel lion an uprising against a government or people in power

re form er someone who works to improve the government or people's lives

re peal to end a law

rep re sen ta tive someone who is chosen to represent, or speak for, others *Voters elect **representatives** to state legislatures.*

res er va tion land set aside for a special purpose *Native Americans were forced to live on **reservations**.*

se cede to break away from an organization, such as a union of states

sec tion a certain part of the country, such as the North or the South; one part of an area

self-gov ern ment government by people who make their own laws and choose their own leaders

set tle to set up home in a new land

tar iff a tax on goods that are brought into a country from another country

ter ror ism the use of violence and fear to control people

trans por ta tion the ways people and goods are carried from one place to another

trea ty an official agreement between countries

vol un teer someone who agrees to serve of his or her own free will

Index Part 1

Congratulations!

You are an informed American. You have learned about the history of America from its first discovery to the years following the Civil War. You now know:

- who the first Americans were and what happened to them;
- who the colonists were and why they came to America;
- how Americans fought to create a nation based on religious freedom, political freedom, individual rights, and democracy;
- how the United States set up a government over 200 years ago that is still working today;
- how immigrants have shaped America and made it what it is today; and
- how Americans throughout the history of this country have worked to bring equal rights and freedom to all Americans.